A Journey of Personal Reflection

SYLVIA CASTILLO

Copyright © 2019 by Sylvia Castillo
All rights reserved. This book or any portion thereof
may not be reproduced or used in any manner whatsoever
without the express written permission of the publisher
except for the use of brief quotations in a book review.
Printed in the United States of America

First Printing, 2019
Editing by Kathy Sparrow
Book design and layout by Honeylette Pino
Chapter illustrations © 2019 Sylvia Castillo
Cover design Copyright © 2019 by Sylvia Castillo & Honeylette Pino

The My Agreements with Me online experience adds so much depth and texture to just reading the book. For a more in-depth and personal experience you are personally invited to Join the Journey.
www.MyAgreementswithMe.com

The SerenitysWay affirmative greeting card and art line are a collection of heart work. Both the affirmative prayers and messages are meaningful and inspiring. The affirmative business solutions are a resource for those wanting to focus on relationships, systems and consistency in their business.
www.SerenitysWay.com

For
Steve, Taylor, Dante, Kamryn & Baileigh

I would not be who I am without you...

Contents

Introduction ix
The Journey Begins 1

1. I make a pact with myself—an agreement with me 6
2. A promise to commit to a more expansive way of being and seeing 10
3. I release the chains of my own bondage 14
4. I know that these agreements afford me the ability to live out my highest truth and vision, and I give thanks for the many blessings that return to me as I embrace my authentic self 18
5. I am impeccable with my word 22
6. and I use my heart and intuition as my guidance 26
7. I pay close attention to when listening is more important than being heard 30
8. and I recognize that the need to understand always takes precedence over the egos demands 34
9. I know that my character, my honesty, and my integrity are all defined by my word 38
10. so I don't make promises that I cannot keep 42
11. I am free to choose in every moment to respond instead of react 46
12. and I vow to never use my words as a weapon or an excuse 50
13. I don't partake in rumors and gossip, for I absolutely know that there is no power or personal growth in the depreciation of another 54
14. I don't take things personally 58

15. I recognize that we are all on a journey—learning, growing, discovering, finding, reaching and figuring out our own plan 62
16. When I stay committed to my highest vision, when I am in integrity with myself, I approach others with patience and humility 66
17. I know that each of us is doing the best we can with our current level of awareness—and I honor that space 70
18. I release all demands and expectations that keep me in judgment..74
19. and I forgive myself and others for our misgivings 78
20. I don't assume anything 82
21. I accept full and total responsibility for my life 86
22. for my relationships, I accept full and total responsibility........90
23. and for my results, I accept full and total responsibility..........94
24. If there is something I need to know, I ask..............................98
25. If there is something I need to say, I communicate................102
26. If there is something missing, I do the best I can to articulate and express who and what I am, and what it is that I need or desire..106
27. There is no story writing 110
28. I will not create my own doubt, animosity, confusion, illusion, bitterness, suspicion, or conflict based on speculation 114
29. I am clear and conscious 118
30. I use my time, my energy, and my voice for resolution and solution..122
31. I am committed to greatness..126
32. I will do the best I can 130
33. and I start with me 134
34. I will love, honor, and nurture, myself..............................138
35. I will take care of my needs..142
36. protect my space (I will) 146
37. expand my consciousness (I will) 150
38. exercise my body and shape my life (I will) 154

39. I will give time to the things that inspire and
    bring joy to me 158
40. I will give all that I have to all that I am committed to.........162
41. I look for opportunities to give of myself,
    my time, and my service 166
42. because I understand the dynamic exchange of giving and
    receiving, and the amazing blessings it brings to my life.......170
43. As I move into this day I carry with me these
    truths and agreements..174
44. and I remember to be gentle along the way..........................178
45. I remember that life is always offering up the opportunity
    for me to be, do, and have everything I desire.....................182
46. I choose yes and let it be so...186
47. And So It Is 190
48. What's next 192
49. Conclusion ~ a Divine message to take with you 196
50. A New Vision 200
51. No Arrival 202

Resources 207
Closing Thoughts 210
Acknowledgements..211
About the Author..212

Introduction

I had no idea that my path would lead me here to write this book. It started with a deep desire and inspired thought to leave a message for someone who really needed to hear the words—"You are worthy. You are enough. Your past does not preceed you. You matter, and you are not alone."

My intention in sharing my thoughts and my heart is to offer a new or different perspective in hopes that a seed of possibility would be planted. We all have "stuff" and how we interpret it and what we do with it, will dictate our actions, affect our results and alter the rest of our lives.

I am no guru and I don't claim to have it all figured out. I have been the victim and I have also been the perpetrator. I think that this life experience offers each one of us an individual journey to love our way through every circumstance and often times we cloud the opportunity with our fear, our judgment and our resistance.

Resistance is deadly and where there is no resistance, there is peace. My hope is that this inward journey of personal reflection would give you a new experience of peace, perspective and possibility.

The Journey Begins

There comes a time when looking outside of ourselves for an explanation, feedback, or an interpretation no longer gives us the resolution we are looking for—because ultimately our answers are within ourselves. No one else's crystal ball, tarot cards or counseling session can see our future or definitively determine why things are the way they are or how they will turn out to be. In the end, it is up to me—to take full and total responsibility for my relationships, for my results, and for my life.

There are four agreements that we have an opportunity to make with ourselves. The *original agreements were given to us by Don Miguel Ruiz, in his book *"The Four Agreements"*. However, there is a deeper exploration of these agreements, and they are *"My Agreements with Me,"* and if you are willing to take an honest look at your own thoughts, behaviors and actions, you could just possibly find answers you were once looking for but could never find. Or even discover things about yourself that you didn't know.

An amazing teacher once said, "We will all get what this life is about, even if it is in our last breath." I believe she meant that life is about the opportunity to live as our True Self, Our Real Self—the one who is powerful, confident, competent, beautiful, strong and worthy in every way. Beyond any circumstance or situation, beyond faults, mistakes, trials or secrets. The one who lives with an open heart—who sees without judgment, who hears without fault, who lives without regret.

As human beings, we are given dominion over our thoughts and experiences, and we choose moment by moment and breath by breath where we will place our attention and how we will see and interpret life. It is this perspective that will determine so much of what we will experience, good or bad, right, wrong, or indifferent. In the end, we will be right about every story and whatever it was that we made up.

It is only through a commitment to our own personal growth and development that we can begin to see if what we've made up is serving the larger vision for our lives. It is in this commitment that we will discover that we are the only ones who can do things different or *be* the change. It is in this journey that we will see what we are under the influence of. And, we get to start right where we are—without judgement. Although we don't necessarily need to uncover deeply buried beliefs to resolve them, sometimes the process gives us an opportunity to be open and vulnerable in a way that serves us when we put it all out there.

For many, there is a certain amount of pain that we will experience because oftentimes pain and contrast to what we really want is the catalyst to move us into a completely different way of "*being*" and "*seeing*." If we are willing to honestly look at it all, we may be freed from chains we never knew we were bound by. My hope is that this journey of self-exploration will provide you with some clarity and or direction as it has for me.

These are the original agreements:

*Be Impeccable with Your Word
*Don't Make Assumptions
*Don't Take Anything Personally
*Always Do Your Best

In *My Agreements with Me,* there is more to look at and contemplate—if you are willing. We will question, explore and discover. There are no right or wrong answers—

There is only your own inherent inner wisdom that will speak to you- guiding, reminding, encouraging and revealing to you your own Truth.

Participation is strongly recommended and the companion *My Agreements with Me* podcast/workbook at MyAgreementswithMe.com will be instrumental in your own personal accountability. It will also give you the opportunity to practice in a way that you might have not ever previously experienced. The weekly podcast will help you maximize this reflective experience. It's a year of reflection—should you choose to make a weekly practice of it. It is definitely up to you, and you can certainly do it your own way, and in your own time, but only if you're ready to look in the mirror.

You may already know that there is another voice that talks to you all the time. The one that lives in your head—sometimes referred to as the crazy roommate, the ego, or the protective personality. It's important that you pay attention. That's the one always finding reasons to back out, sleep in, make excuses, or give up. It's the one that feels anxious, depressed, scared, weak, limited, and unworthy. It's also the one that will tell you that there's nothing left to do because you have already arrived. For those who have done some personal growth work, sometimes there is an idea that the work is done. Don't believe it. Life is a continual journey of expansion regardless of where you are on the journey and regardless of your name, career, education, socioeconomic status, gender, color, background, or sexual orientation.

Your True Self, the Real Self that I spoke of earlier, doesn't play in the arena of lack and limitation. There is always growth and expansion from wherever we are. We have dominion over our thoughts, and we are free to choose in every moment. Sometimes we think that the True/Real Self has left or gone MIA (missing in action), but the Truth is that our True/Real Self is always there—in all ways and all the time, patiently waiting. And it will wait, and wait, and wait, even for a lifetime for us to get realigned, back to center, and authentically on course. That is the beauty, the power the mystery, and the trip of free will. We get to be right about everything—every thought, every idea, every opinion, belief, conclusion, illusion, suggestion, projection, or interpretation we make up.

Maybe it's time to look in the mirror?

Notes and Reflections

My Agreements with Me

I make a pact with myself— an agreement with me. A promise to commit to a more expansive way of being and seeing. I release the chains of my own bondage. I know that these agreements afford me the ability to live out my highest truth and vision, and I give thanks for the many blessings that return to me as I embrace my authentic self.

I am impeccable with my word, and I use my heart and intuition as my guidance. I pay close attention to when listening is more important than being heard, and I recognize that the need to understand always takes precedence over the egos demands. I know that my character, my honesty, and my integrity are all defined by my word so I don't make promises that I cannot keep. I am free to choose in every moment to respond instead of react, and I vow to never use my words as a weapon or an excuse. I don't partake in rumors and gossip, for I absolutely know that there is no power or personal growth in the depreciation of another.

I don't take things personally. I recognize that we are all on a journey—learning, growing, discovering, finding, reaching, and figuring out our own plan. When I stay committed to my highest vision, when I am in integrity with myself, I approach others with patience and humility. I know that each of us is doing the best we can with our current level of awareness— and I honor that space. I release all demands and expectations that keep me in judgment, and I forgive myself and others for our misgivings.

I don't assume anything. I accept full and total responsibility for my life, for my relationships, and for my results. If there is something I need to know, I ask. If there is something I need to say, I communicate. If there is something missing, I do the best I can to articulate and express who and what I am, and what it is that I need or desire. There is no story writing; I will not create my own doubt, animosity, confusion, illusion, bitterness, suspicion, or conflict based on spectulation. I am clear and conscious- I use my time, my energy, and my voice for resolution and solution. I am committed to greatness.

I will do the best I can, and I start with me. I will love, honor, and nurture myself. I will take care of my needs, protect my space, expand my consciousness, exercise my body, and shape my life. I will give time to the things that inspire and bring joy to me. I will give all that I have to all that I am committed to. I will look for opportunities to give of myself, my time, and my service because I understand the dynamic exchange of giving and receiving, and the amazing blessings it brings to my life.

As I move into this day, I carry with me these truths and agreements, and I remember to be gentle along the way. I remember that life is always offering up the opportunity for me to be, do and have everything I desire. I choose yes and let it be so. And so it is~

~*Sylvia Castillo*

1. I make a pact with myself— an agreement with me

This is where it all starts. It's an agreement you have with yourself and it's not about anyone or anything else. It's not about right or wrong or good or bad. It's simply an opportunity to be real with yourself and to start right where you are—to honestly take an inventory of your life and your results and to determine where there are things in your life that are ready to grow.

A "pact" is a solemn and sacred agreement that you make with yourself. As you contemplate what that might be, remember that this journey is about you. This is not about your parents, children, spouse, friends, or significant other. It's about you. Now would be the time to release their influences and ideas about who and what you should be. This agreement is for you and you alone. It is a journey of self-discovery, and all that is needed is you and your willingness to explore.

So, what is the agreement or pact you have with yourself? And do you even have one? Maybe you don't. This might be the first time that an agreement with yourself has ever been suggested. It is also possible that you've been getting by day to day, doing life, and feeling just fine about where you are. Or you may have been so consumed with taking care of everyone and everything else, that you never really thought about yourself or what agreement you might have with you. Maybe you have goals and those are your agreements? They might be written down, memorized, and tracked, although there are other areas that you struggle with. Either way, the opportunity here is to create some agreements that you would like to make and keep with yourself.

Taking the time to write out your thoughts and new agreements with yourself has more benefits than you could possibly know. When you use your imagination and creativity to design and craft a vision that gets you excited, when you can feel yourself tingling on the inside with the possibility of it all, your vision begins working on how to find its way to you.

When you begin to deliberately create new agreements with yourself, you ignite a spark of probability that has within it the power to make real that which you could only conceive of. Don't make light of this opportunity. If you could know the power of writing down your thoughts and your words, you would want to make sure you took time for this exercise. If you could wave the magic wand, what might you have more, better, new, or different in your life?

It doesn't matter if you do or do not currently have a vision for your life, or if this conversation is new to you or not. This is an important invitation for you to start this journey of self-discovery wherever you are on your path.

These are the major areas in our lives that we explore. If you could have it any way you wanted it, what would it look and feel like? Take the time to write out a vision for your life. Include everything.

Health/Wellbeing * Relationships * Career/ Education * Contribution/Spirituality

Your vision is the big picture. It is your roadmap including your dreams and desires. You can write it as though it's five years in the future, and you are looking back at all of the amazing things you have accomplished, or you can state it "as if" in the present tense. It is encouraged that you spend some quality time thinking about what you would have in your life. You don't need to know how or why. Just get clear about what you'd like to have and create and get excited about it. We are setting a stage for the future you.

*For additional insight and maximum results, join the companion My Agreements with Me podcast/workbook at MyAgreementswithMe.com

Notes and Reflections

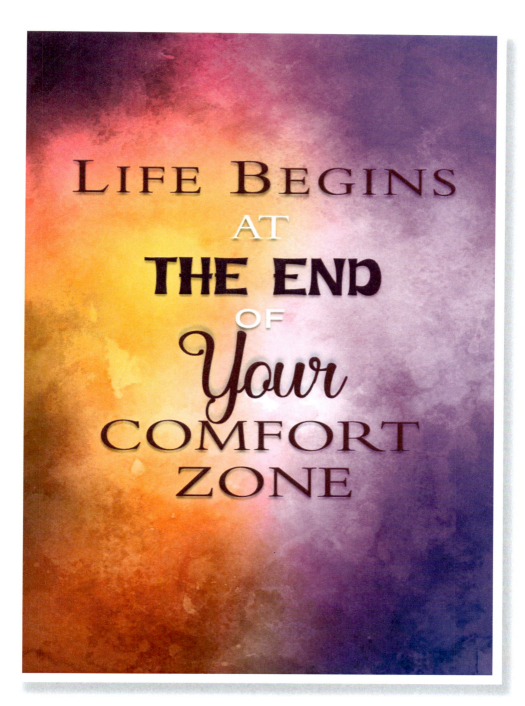

2. A promise to commit to a more expansive way of being and seeing

To be expansive is to be far-reaching and inclusive. It means to move beyond your current level of comfortability. One of the ways we get comfortable is to stay inclusive with only the people we know. In being expansive in the way that you see others, there could be an opportunity to create new and lasting relationships with people you may have never given a chance. Being expansive in your ways of *being* and *seeing* would open doors, build bridges, and give you even more opportunities and experiences to meet amazing people.

Sometimes we tend to see things in only one particular way or think that others should believe in the same things we believe in. Often times we judge others that they are wrong and damned if they don't follow the same path that we do. We make assumptions about who they are and what they stand for, and frankly, we don't know the first thing about them. We judge according to appearances, and we assume. We generally operate from the standpoint of I'm right and you're wrong.

Experimenting in this life is like having your own laboratory. You get the opportunity to test out new ways of being to see how you show up and to see how your BEingness affects others. You get to research, question, explore, and discover what works and what doesn't.

Most of the time we are on auto-pilot, waking up on the same side of the bed, eating and drinking the same thing for breakfast, driving the same way to work, doing the same routine at work, coming home for dinner, and watching tv only to repeat it again tomorrow. We think the same thoughts, hang out with the same people, and do the same things over and over and over.

When was the last time you did something new or decided to have an experience that was uncomfortable, pushed your limits, or gave yourself an opportunity to consider another perspective? The opportunity here is to notice what you're thinking. Are you excited or irritated at the idea of doing something different? What is your self-talk, and are you being closed or open-minded?

Being committed to a more expansive way of being and seeing looks like something will feel different. It means to purposely have new experiences. It's doing things you haven't done, talking with people that generally you would describe as not your kind of people. It's having coffee with a neighbor, dancing when you don't dance, singing karaoke when you don't sing. It's volunteering or visiting church with a different set of values. It's repairing a broken relationship, going on a blind date, or skydiving.

Beginning to do things that are outside of being comfortable is the start of creating things that are new and different. There will be a part of you that says, "I'm not going to do that. It's stupid." You will come up against the voice of your own protective personality, the excuses will show up immediately, and you will create every reason to give up or not start. The protective personality wants to keep you safe, and anything that is new or different will feel like a threat. It will be fearful, and you will have to make a conscious choice to say "Yes" anyway.

Be risky today! Commit to being honest and vulnerable. Hold yourself accountable to being and doing something different. Do something that involves other people and don't hide out. Have an experience outside of your comfort zone. Once a decision is made to grow and you choose to **Believe**, anything is possible.

Notes and Reflections

Believe

Everything about your vision still holds true...
for the way you wish to be in the world
and for all the ways in which you shine your light.
It's an ongoing process of self-discovery...
You know there are adjustments that need to be made,
and you're making them.
Your devotion to your highest truth and your dedication
to your ongoing health and well-being,
keep you in the flow of good.
There are no mistakes and you are here on purpose—
powerfully co-creating this amazing life.
I know that you are attracting to you everything you need
for the fulfillment of your vision.
Your commitment to surround yourself
with joy, love, honesty, and integrity-
keep your path open to greater and greater possibility.
You have everything you need
and you are seeded with the perfection of Spirit.
Remember you need only to turn within.

Sylvia Castillo

3. I release the chains of my own bondage

If you were being guided by your own inner wisdom and guidance, what would be the message? Is there something that sits on your heart like a weight? Are there things that you have wanted to do or express that you don't? Are there desires in you that you are ignoring?

Your desires of your True/Real Self are born of the heart. They are the things that live within you that are always there. Passions that are unexplored, ideas unexpressed, inventions not made, music not played, books yet to be written, songs not sung, and experiences not had.

You are here as an original blessing—perfect, whole, and complete. What stands between you and your highest good are your own thoughts and limiting ideas and beliefs about yourself. These patterns of thinking have touched all of our lives in some way.

> I'm not safe.
> I don't belong.
> I'm not smart enough.
> I'm not loved.
> I'm not good enough.
> I'm not important.
> I don't have anything to contribute.
> I will be alone.

Your hesitations of moving forward in the areas where you desire growth and expansion are rooted in fear. They are generally programs that were put in place early in your life. They are old and outdated. They are voices and memories of the past, and they keep you bound.

When you are ready to explore, and you want more for your life, you will be ready to write a new story for your future. A commitment to being uncomfortable will be needed as you move away from the safety and security of the walls you have built around yourself.

Writing a new story.

Write down your story and your experience in any area of your life where you have felt betrayed, victimized, offended, abused, or violated. Now, take full and total responsibility for any part that you may have played or choices you made—including ignoring red flags, clues, or a knowingness that things were off course.

Instead of asking, "Why me? What's wrong with me? Who's to blame?"

Ask, "Who am I when I'm strong and powerful? What is wanting to be birthed? What gifts do I have to give to the world? How much power can flow through me? What is my next step?"

As you consider what is wanting to be birthed, recognize that it is impossible for you to move forward while you are still holding on to the past. Be focused on forgiveness to anyone or anything that has kept you in a place of ongoing judgement.

Write down everyone and everything that is unforgiven and include anyone, anything or any condition that needs to be forgiven. **Release** the past and anyone or anything that you have used as an excuse that keeps you in bondage. After you have read the list of unforgivenessess, burn the list and once and for all choose to let it go so that you can focus on a new vision for your life.

I Release, and I let go

Notes and Reflections

Release

No longer will I be consumed
by this sorrow and pain.
From this moment forward,
I choose to use my heart as my compass.
To go within,
to be guided by my inner
wisdom and knowledge.
and to accept myself just as I am.
I choose this day to be free.
free from my past,
free from my ego,
and free from every thought
that has kept me
from my highest good.
Today I release all pain,
all anger and all frustration.
Today I step into the Me
that I was designed to Be.

Sylvia Castillo

4. I know that these agreements afford me the ability to live out my highest truth and vision, and I give thanks for the many blessings that return to me as I embrace my authentic self

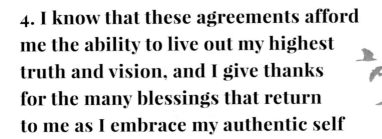

Being "Authentic" means you are real and genuine and not a copy, and by the way, you are not meant to be anyone else.

You are an original blessing, and you are here purposefully and powerfully—whether you recognize that or not. You have free will and dominion over your thoughts and actions, and you are always at choice to follow your inner guidance or not—and just because you are not following it, does not mean it doesn't exist.

Regarding authenticity—when we are authentic, what we think, say, feel, and do are in alignment. In other words, you don't say "yes" when you really mean "no." You don't agree to participate with a smile on your face when inside you are angry and in resentment.

When you are authentic, you can respectfully decline. You are able to speak your truth without making others wrong about their truth. You can give your opinion without second guessing yourself, and you are able to accept constructive criticism without being offended because you know that the feedback will ultimately make you better. Imagine not making other people responsible for the way you feel or feeling like you don't matter or don't belong.

When you are living an authentic life, you are on a path that you are proud to call your own, and you are with people that you honestly enjoy being with. It is a mutual experience of give, take, and compromise—and it feels good. Our internal guidance is always talking to us; gently nudging us to listen to the answers we intuitively know are within. If you don't feel you are living authentically, if you are not on track with the highest vision for your life, you may be feeling anxiety, depression, and sadness.

Your highest Truth is that you are Perfect, Whole, and Complete. You are not broken, unworthy, or incapable. The challenge for many of us is that we don't embrace who we are. We have this idea that something is missing and that we don't measure up.

For many there is no vision, no goals, no plan, and no purpose.

There is an epidemic going on—a shortage of vision, a disconnection with a higher power and purpose, a disembodiment and the feeling of not being connected in your own skin. There is a sense of victimization, ongoing feelings of depression, anxiety, fear, and separation—and many have decided that the solution is opioids, prescription drugs, painkillers, alcohol, and the many other ways we numb out, check out, and turn off.

In many cases, our focus is in the wrong place. Whatever you place your attention and intention on will grow and whatever you disregard will slowly eat away at you.

"If I were speaking my truth, what would I be saying? Who would I be supporting? Where would I be serving? What would by life's message be? What would be my legacy?"

What we focus on expands. Write it out, plan it out, and spell it out—even if it seems far-fetched and unreachable.

When we take 100% responsibility for our lives, it includes a vision. A vision is an invitation into imagination and inspiration. It is an opportunity to co-create beyond appearances, excuses, failures, mistakes or regrets. It is the power of anticipating that which may or will come to be.

What is the **Vision** for your life?

I am going to write it as though I am looking back 5 years from now or in the present tense—I am going to write it from a place of thanks and gratitude for all the ways my life is exciting and fulfilling.

What would my life look like? Who would be in it? What would I have done? Where would I have been? Who are the incredible people

I have met? What would I have seen? What would I have experienced and accomplished? How does it feel? This new vision for my life will be my focus and my commitment. It is where I will include my desires and it is where I will place my attention and intention.

After the vision is created, begin to create a blueprint for the actions necessary to have the things that are desired. So, if it's a better body you are wanting, maybe you need a membership to the gym, work-out partner, an eating plan, or dietary supplements?

Consider at least one thing in each of the areas of your life. Set Specific, Measurable, Attainable, Risky, Timely (SMART) goals. Give yourself the gift of putting yourself first and staying the course. This is a commitment to grow in ways you didn't know were possible and **It Is Time**.

it is time

It is time for letting go.
It is time to release the pain.
It is time to lay down every excuse
and rediscover
this thing called You.
Breaking down every barrier,
laying down every judgment
and casting out all
fear, doubt and separation.
It is time
to embrace your truth.
It is time
to begin again.
It is time
to rise up, to turn within,
time to own your power and discover
every possibility, to recognize every gift
and step into the you
that was meant to be.
It is time.

Sylvia Castillo

5. I am impeccable with my word

Impeccable means to be in accordance with the highest standards, to be faultless. We are human, so being faultless is probably not realistic; however, how is your relationship with your word? Does your word have the highest standard and what does that even mean? Long before paper contracts, agreements were made, and deals were done on your word. A handshake was a verbal commitment, and a man (or woman) was only as good as his or her word.

If you told someone you would take care of something, they would never worry or second guess about whether it would actually happen, because you would make sure of it, no matter what. There wasn't a question or discussion; it was just handled.

Imagine that same commitment in your everyday life—when you told your spouse you would call them right back, or when you promised your child you would play with them in five minutes. Maybe you mentioned to a co-worker you would help out or made an agreement with a friend you would be there at a certain time. Can the people who know you trust your word? Do you do what you say you're going to do?

The foundation for a word that is impeccable is trust and integrity. When you are or decide to be a man or woman of your word, there is a shift in the level of respect you receive from others and the amount of respect you have for yourself. This is not to say that you will be perfect all time; however, you will do whatever it takes to keep your word, and if for some reason you must break your word, you communicate to get on the same page and get back in alignment with your word.

There was a man that once had a business; many people worked for him in different roles and in multiple pay scales although everyone wanted a "special arrangement" with him for one reason or another. The man promised everyone that his agreement was black and white, on a contract that it was the same for everyone. Over time though he found different reasons and excuses to make those "special arrangements." In the end, the price he paid was losing of his company and relationships because he failed to be a man of his word.

There are prices we pay for breaking our word, and there are also the prices others pay for us breaking our word.

What about your word with yourself? For many people, it is here where they have an even bigger challenge of keeping their word. What have you been wanting to do that you haven't been able to keep your word with yourself? Where have you fallen short when it comes to you? Self-care is usually one of the first things that are given up in order to take care of everyone else. How is your word with you?

This is your opportunity and your year to really look at yourself and your commitments, to really look in the mirror at your own behaviors, your self-talk, your vision and your word with yourself.

Declare the following: I will be devoted to paying attention. To writing down and paying close attention to where I am breaking my word with myself and others. The first thing I will look at is my journey with this process *My Agreements with Me.*

How have I done over the previous four weeks? In thirty days, have I been able to compete the four exercises? Did I set some goals and ask for accountability? Did I attempt to expand my way of being and seeing by doing something uncomfortable or unfamiliar? Did I do the forgiveness work and release and let go of something that was holding me back? Have I created a vision for my life?

No one else is responsible for your success or failure and this process gives you an opportunity to be real with yourself. Are you willing to create a better relationship with your word?

What if all that was needed was your personal faith in your own ability to trust yourself and to honor your own word and your life? What would be possible?

Notes and Reflections

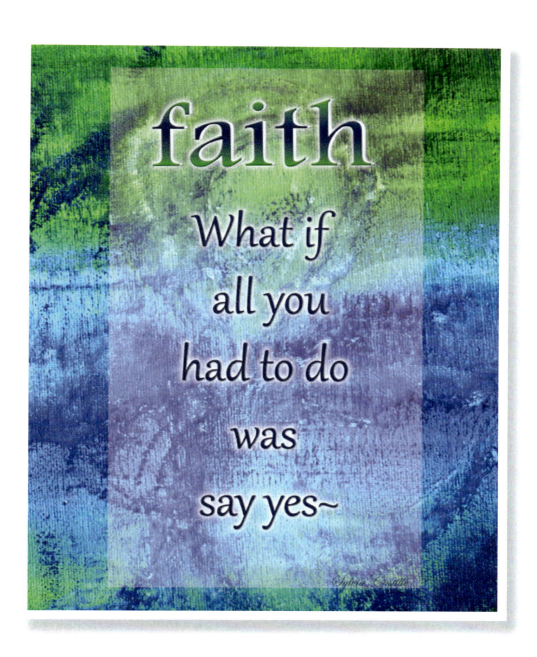

6. and I use my heart and intuition as my guidance

A man boards a train with his two children, and although they are nicely dressed, their behavior seems to be a bit unruly. They are running and jumping and not paying much attention to the elderly lady sitting near the front with her book. As they continue to run and laugh and play, another passenger approaches their father to ask him if he could do something about the kids. The father turned to the passenger and politely said, "I understand that they are a little overbearing however their mother just passed away and this is the first time I've heard them laugh in a couple of weeks. If it's ok with you, I'd rather not say anything."

In an instant, our perspective is shifted. The circumstance did not change, the environment was the same, and the only thing different was that for a moment we moved from our thinking mind into our heart.

It's amazing that we have the power to do this in each and every single moment. We don't need an excuse, we don't need a story or a reason—we can simply choose to change our frame of reference. Can you imagine how powerful that could be if we made an intentional practice of using our heart and intuition as our guidance system?

There is an opportunity to really pay attention to where in the body you feel the first signs of something going south. There will only be a split second to make a conscious decision, to locate where in the body there is dis-ease (upset) and take a deep breath. You could actually dissolve the negative energy and shift in the very moment that something was coming up.

The patterning of the mind is to label what we feel, to name it and blame it, to make the cause of our problem outside of ourselves. Immediately, when that happens, our thinking mind has completely taken over. For some it could be several hours, days, months, or years—and even a lifetime to move back into the heart.

We will defend and argue for our limitations, so much evidence to be right and righteous, so many memories to stay in unforgiveness. The walls get taller and taller, and the heart gets buried and trapped in all of that pain and negative energy.

The reality of a protected heart is burned bridges, broken relationships, and deep unforgiveness. It plays out in our homes and in our lives as arguments, chaos, disease, ailments, fights, war, depression, addiction, and suicide.

It is written that our mind was always supposed to be a servant to our hearts, and yet, they say that the longest distance is that 12-18 inch journey. The sad truth is that some people never take the journey, and the crazy thing is that you would never know. Everything looks great on the outside—Cover it, mask it, hide it and live behind this false perception that everything is ok when the truth is that something is longing to be freed.

Intuition is another amazing gift we have. We are able to actually know things without conscious reasoning—we just know… What would happen if we had a practice of trusting our gut, our inklings, and nudges? What if we made a decision to call that person when they crossed our mind or say hello to that person that we felt a connection to. What if in the moment of frustration, we decided to breath and anchor in such a way that we were not just reacting and defending.

Say to yourself: I will commit to using my heart and intuition as my guidance. I will keep one eye on the inside—consciously and mindfully practicing to anchor in my heart and to allow that to be my guidance. Deeply rooted in a place of peace. I **Choose Love**.

Notes and Reflections

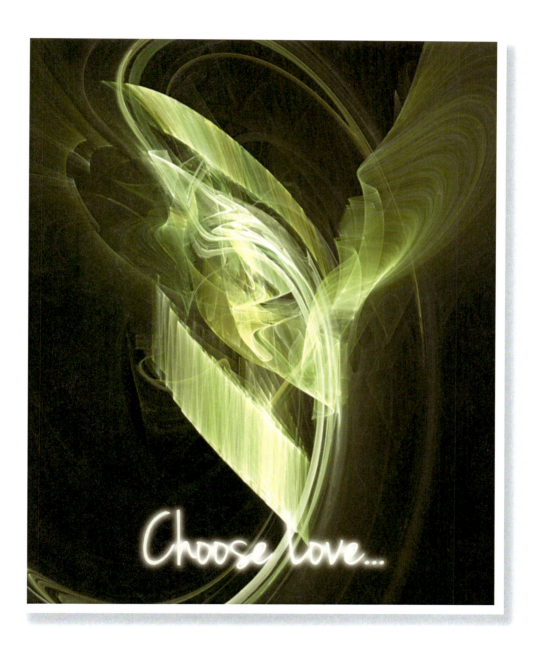

7. I pay close attention to when listening is more important than being heard

Of all the opportunities we have to learn about ourselves and others, listening is probably the greatest of them all.

Can you listen in such a way that the person speaking really feels like you "get them?" That you were with them through the entire conversation—and not caught up in what amazing response, or advice you might give them, not agreeing or disagreeing, or finding some commonality so that you can relate. Can you listen without checking your Facebook, Twitter, or Snapchat? Can you just *Be Present* for the person sitting in front of you?

Each tends to listen with our strongly held positions, views, opinions, judgments and justifications without really ever being fully available to explore and discover. Any time that we have the idea or thought that "I already know what you're going to say," we have diminished the opportunity to understand and engage in "authentic listening."

When we assume, draw conclusions, worry, disapprove, or judge we miss the experience of truly being able to leave someone feeling as though we really "get them,"—and any time we enter a conversation thinking that we have someone else's answers, or that it is our job to solve their problem(s), we are off track with the gift of authentic listening.

Imagine what it would look like if we went in to every conversation assuming that we have something to learn? What if we asked open ended questions and really practiced the idea of "seek first to understand." Can you imagine what might be possible for someone to open up and share if they did not feel that they would feel judged or condemned? What if you offered a space of trust and acceptance for whatever might be said? We couldn't even begin to know the blessing of what it might be like for another person to share their most intimate and vulnerable feelings—to *be* the presence of love for another is one of the most generous and selfless gifts we have to offer.

The opportunity here is not only in paying attention to how we show up as a listener with others, but also to recognize traits within ourselves. How do I communicate with others? Am I the one who dominates every conversation? Do I always have something to say?

Am I talking without any regard for others? Am I the wallflower who is just about invisible with nothing to say? Do I have to argue to get my point across? Do others want to talk with me? There is no right or wrong answer. It's just an opportunity to recognize, to pay attention, and ask if how you are showing up is in alignment with the greater vision you have for your life?

Who in your life needs you to listen? Decide to be thoughtful in the way that you will listen. Approach each interaction and conversation with the thought that you have something to learn or gain from listening authentically. Seek first to understand, whether it's a conversation with you friend, co-worker, spouse, or child. Decide today to be authentic and to accept everyone for who they are and where they are. Turn the radio down, turn the tv off, put your phone away. Grab a glass of wine or orange juice, and a comfy pair of socks, get cozy, and decide to connect with someone in a beautiful and powerful way. It really is that simple.

Notes and Reflections

8. and I recognize that the need to understand always takes precedence over the egos demands

Let's talk about the ego and its demands; it's demands are that you do not experience anything new or outside of your comfort zone. The ego is designed to keep you safe, and it is all about survival. The moment you have a thought or an idea to do something outside of your "normal," it will go to work to fight against it. Resistance will begin immediately.

Have you ever decided to do something new or different, and the moment you made a decision to "do the thing," the voices of fear, doubt, rejection, and resistance immediately kicked in.

In the book *The War of Art,* Stephen Pressfield explains how "Resistance is self-generated and self-perpetuated. It is described as the enemy within (a/k/a the crazy roommate). He says that resistance is insidious and that it will tell you anything to keep you from doing your work. It will perjure, fabricate, falsify seduce, bully, cajole. Resistance is protean. It will assume any form, it that is what it takes to deceive you. It will reason with you like a lawyer or jam a nine-millimeter in your face like a stickup man. Resistance has no conscience. It will pledge anything to get a deal, then double-cross you as soon as your back is turned. If you take Resistance at its word, you deserve everything you get. Resistance is always lying and always full of shit."

Our job is not to figure out how to remove, numb out, or hide the ego or resistance. It is truly an opportunity to go deep, and in many instances to move beyond our fearful protective personality. It's helpful to understand that that the ultimate goal of the ego is to protect us from any harm or perceived danger. When we can see our own resistance from a loving and compassionate place, we can actually end the struggle. It will however require us to wake up, to be conscious in our decision making, to look within the heart for guidance, and to open to the mystery and the power of forgiveness.

Forgiveness by the way is essential. It's impossible to move forward when we are holding onto the past. Sometimes we think we have forgiven someone or something, and the sure way to tell is to bring that person to mind, to see, talk with or about the person, or situation. If there is any negative energy, bad feelings, or unpleasant emotion that comes up in the body, there is still healing work to do.

And what about understanding? We are so quick to judge and condemn others. To understand is to learn and to have knowledge, to see another side or perspective. To stand in another's shoes. Somewhere it is said that life is *always* conspiring for my greater good. This would mean that even in the face of uncertainty, or things I cannot explain, there is a purpose that may be beyond my own interpretation or understanding.

The opportunity that lies just under Forgiveness is the most important and essential work we will ever do. It's so easy to write people off, place blame, and point fingers. We make a judgment and a decision about someone or something and we're done—never to look back. For some this means no mom or dad, a loss of siblings and friends, kids tied up in the middle of their parent's issues, and on and on and on. It is drug addiction, sexual addictions, food addictions—it is falling out, numbing out and checking out.

What if in the revealing of another's pain and perspective, we had within it the ability to heal our perception? What if right at the point of understanding and forgiveness, we were able to create new ways of communicating? What if the possibility of alchemy was one tender moment or one loving decision away?

Our job is not to be the judge and jury—it is to be the witness.

What relationship in your life could possibly shift with a dose of understanding and forgiveness? Where in your life do you need to forgive yourself and where can you be more forgiving of others? The practice is week is forgiveness—of myself and others. It is not a practice of cutting others out of my life, it is the willingness to give as before.

Notes and Reflections

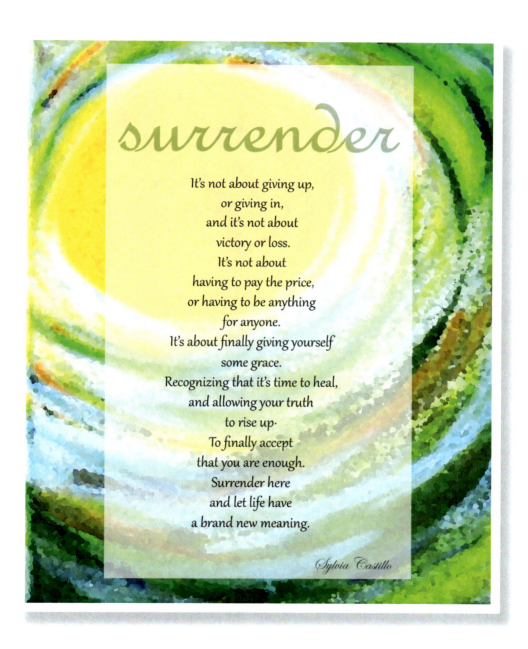

9. I know that my character, my honesty, and my integrity are all defined by my word

Let's see if we can dive a little deeper into the meaning here. Character is related to morals, and morals are knowing the difference between right and wrong.

Honesty is about truthfulness, sincerity, and having a freedom from fraud, while integrity is about the steady devotion to these principles.

The opportunity here is to go within—to look in the mirror at yourself and your word—the words you use with yourself and others, the integrity you either have or don't have, and your honesty around everything—from the little white lie to completely deceiving and dishonoring myself and others.

Whenever there is a contradiction in what you say or how you feel, that's the opportunity for growth.

This is certainly not to be taken lightly; there are extreme prices to pay when we find ourselves in the middle of circumstances that remind us that we are not on track. The contrast can be unimaginably painful, and yet, it is an amazing blessing to be able to look at the evidence and results of life and to be able to make a conscious decision to stay on a path that perpetuates mediocrity or to draw a line in the sand.

Ask yourself: What are the morals I stand for? How do I stand in my own truth even in the face of adversity or others who may not have a standard in their own lives? What am I willing to risk, lose, or walk away from to stand for something? No one has the answers to these questions except you. Maybe it's easier to not have a standard and to just go with the flow. Although, somehow, I think the soul knows. It's the constant reminder that we're off track—the dull pain, the subtle ache, the little whisper, or the big red truck.

Are you a healer, coach, or advisor who is out of alignment with your own words and teaching?

Are you a sales person who's in it just for the buck?

Are you a dentist who is pulling teeth when your patient has no ailment or sign of decay? (Yes, this is a real thing.)

Are you a giving more time to your distractions than your family?

Are you a wife who is lying to your husband about where money is being spent?

Are you playing catfish because you're not ok with who you are?

Are your addictions so out of control that you have completely lost yourself?

Is it painful to be in your skin? Do you need to pop a pill just to get through the day? Or do you end each night with a drink or several so you can sleep.

Maybe it's a little more subtle: are you in a marriage where you spend most of your time alone? Is he in front of the TV while you are managing everything else? Do you feel that her friends are more important than your needs? Are you just surviving and/or getting by?

We know the answers intuitively.

There comes a time when being out of alignment no longer serves you—when the decision to be in complete integrity with yourself means that you are ready to trust God, the process, the Universe, Spirit, Jesus, Buddha, Father-Mother (whatever you call it) and also trust that life is *always* conspiring for our greater good, and that there is a power in the Universe and we can use it.

Are you willing to have a conversation with yourself about your word? Are you willing to go deeper—to check yourself on your honesty? Can you be devoted to being the witness? To really pay attention to how you're showing up?

What if your word was everything? What if your dreams are waiting for you to get in integrity with your word?

Notes and Reflections

10. so I don't make promises that I cannot keep

A promise is a declaration or assurance that one will do a particular thing or that a particular thing will happen. Have you noticed that we tend to make promises all of the time? A promise is a vow that I will keep my word—that I will pledge my word and guarantee that I will commit, declare, and definitely do what I promised. It's a covenant and it's intended to be sacred.

Think about the potential that lies in making a promise—the absolute power in giving your word and making a promise to a particular thing. What would life and our relationships look like if we kept the promises we made?

I promise to love you for better or for worse, for richer or for poorer, in sickness and in health, in good times and bad as long as we both shall live. Before we explore this area of promises, it would never be assumed or expected that one would stay in a commitment where there was abuse. **"The average length of a marriage that ends in divorce is 8 years-41% of first marriages end in divorce, 60% of second marriages end in divorce and 73% of third marriages end in divorce." The statistics are not in our favor.

Are we entering into a sacred promise and commitment completely unprepared? Do we have false expectations about what a marriage or a committed relationship is supposed to look like? Are we making another person responsible for our own happiness or well-being?

* *https://www.wf-lawyers.com/divorce-statistics-and-facts/*
** *https://www.mckinleyirvin.com/Family-Law-Blog/2012/October/32-Shocking-Divorce-Statistics.aspx*

Are we completely missing the experience to learn and grow with another human being in a sacred commitment and with someone who is absolutely going to give us the opportunity to participate in feeling every emotion that we have the capacity to feel? Is there a possibility that what lies just beneath forgiveness is an intimacy, an integrity, and a wisdom that we could have never known without the experience of shame, regret, or hurt?

We run from one person to another looking for perfection, acting as though the most important quality of what one has to offer is a pedigree, a bank balance, or a collection of things, and yet, much of our population lives with anxiety, fear, depression, sadness, and pain.

Is it possible that there is another way to move through this or any promise or commitment with someone else or with ourselves? A way that requires forgiveness, compassion, understanding, acceptance, and truly unconditional love?

And what about the rest of our relationships? Those with our children, siblings, and friends. Do we just write them off as well? Again, there is no suggestion that we should not create boundaries, and yet, it appears we could be missing out entirely on an opportunity to experience a profound intimacy (into me I see) in the rawness, the realness, the vulnerability, and the entirety of another human being—the good, the bad, and the ugly. With all of our faults, fears, dreams, joys, failures, and accomplishments. You can rest assured that we will have them all.

So, what if we approached "The Promise" from an unfamiliar perspective? What if the promise was to yourself. Declare: I will first make a promise with myself and make the focus of my attention me, not in a selfish kind of way. If I take care of me first, that if I resolve to heal every unforgiveness, then I would experience you from a completely different place.

Notes and Reflections

The Promise

I DO solemnly resolve before Spirit, my higher power, by what ever name that has meaning to me— to take full responsibility for my life, for my relationships, and for my results.

I WILL grow in all areas of my life, and I promise not to leave this planet having regrets about things I didn't do. I understand that I am important; an indispensable, unique, one-of-a-kind original. There is no one else like me and my gifts and contributions to this world are essential.

I WILL make a promise to myself to be the best version of me that I can possibly be and to be a Spiritual leader of my home.

I WILL follow My Agreements with Me. I will be impeccable with my word. I will not take things personally. I won't assume anything, and I will do the best I can.

I WILL live a life of integrity, leading with purpose and honor.

I WILL teach my family with values, principles, and unconditional love.

I WILL cultivate an environment of strength and trust inside and outside of my home. I will build upon our character and treat others with kindness, respect, and compassion.

I WILL work diligently, and I will be a good steward of my resources, my time, my energy and my money.

I WILL practice forgiveness and resolve to heal every wounded place within me.

I WILL be a person of my word, creating a vision for my life and using my time to fulfill my Promise.

_____
Signature   Date

_____   _____
Witness   Date   Witness   Date

11. I am free to choose in every moment to respond instead of react

Responding and reacting are very different ways of approaching a conversation, a challenge, or a situation. Responding means that I have listened, processed, and thought about a response and possibly replied and gave feedback. Where reacting generally has lots of emotion and energy. Typically there is no thought and, it is usually followed by an outburst or an eruption of words full of venom and then an apology or regret.

Have you ever stopped to ask yourself why there are certain people, phrases and/or moments that "set you off?" It's almost as though you don't have any self-control and that all of the self-development, or self-control you thought you had was suddenly lost.

Generally, we find every reason to judge, blame, and find excuses as to why "that person" is the cause for my upset or my inability to reason or respond, and although we can go our entire lifetime with that kind of a perspective, there is an opportunity to look at "those people" and "those events" as an opportunity to go inward to investigate.

If there is negative energy around someone specific when you think about them, or if you find yourself unable to feel grounded because of all the things going on around you, it might be a good time to be mindful about how often that is happening. If you find yourself yelling all of the time to get your point across, or if getting mad and loud is your way of being heard, it is possible that it's time to take a look at that too.

We tend to spend most of our time in our heads—figuring things out, analyzing, judging, condemning, justifying, controlling, projecting, and resisting what is.

Being mindful and paying attention to what is going on **in our thought process, how were thinking, feeling, and reacting is really the beginning of awakening.**

Being able to respond instead of react is a result of feeling grounded and safe. It has to do with feeling anchored in our physical body and in our own truth—and not feeling like we are controlled by those things around us or things that are out of our control. There are certainly many practices for feeling grounded, although meditation, prayer, and breathwork tend to be among the most effective.

Meditation and stillness is such an incredible practice, and when made a priority, it is life-changing. When we go within, when we take time to be still and anchor to that greater something (the power that is literally breathing and sustaining us in each and every moment), we feel a sense of belonging and purpose that does not—and cannot—come from the outside world, or the acceptance or approval of others.

Interestingly enough, our ability to respond to another from a kind and loving perspective, or even to be neutral and to see a situation from more than one vantage point is related to this sense of connectedness, just as an inability to respond is related to a disconnectedness.

Declare: This week I pay attention to how often I respond and/or react to others, especially around the unexpected. Do I flow with or am I resistant? Am I a team player or in my head am I projecting feelings of anger or rage? How do I feel in my body? Is there pain? Am I feeling contracted? Am I willing to pay attention to what is happening with me?

Do I spend more time in my head than anywhere else? How am I BEing?

Today I am willing to begin a practice in one of the three areas of either meditation, prayer, or breathwork, taking at least fifteen minutes per day to be still. My commitment is to pay attention to how I BE.

Notes and Reflections

Be Vibrant Be Brilliant
Be a Leader **Be First**
Be Loving
Be Kind
Be Courageous
Be Willing **BE RISKY**
Be Bold
Be Joyful
BE GRATEFUL
Be Giving
Believe!

Sylvia Castillo

12. and I vow to never use my words as a weapon or an excuse

A weapon is a thing that is designed for injury or bodily harm, a means for gaining an advantage, and an excuse is used to defend or justify. Most of us have experienced a full-blown argument where the words felt as though they were actually inflicting physical pain.

Things said that could never be taken back and some things said will be remembered for a lifetime because of the intensity of the words and the feelings they elicited. We often carry internal scars that feel as though they will never heal. Some will spend the rest of their lives attempting to figure out what is wrong them or why they don't matter; others will build walls or steel cages and vow to never forgive or let anyone in—meanwhile hating the reality they are living in.

Isn't it interesting how one moment can shape an entire life? It is amazing how much power our word has—the power of a thousand suns someone once said. The power to create, the power to heal, the power to forgive and accept, and equally there is a power to shame, blame, hurt, manipulate, deify and destroy.

There is a relentless voice, the one that lives in our heads—the one that we hear when no one is around. It is the voice that was programmed long before we knew that it would control the way we see the world—the voice that defines, defends and argues for every limitation. It does everything in its power to keep us safe, small and quiet. Never to be seen or heard.

Meanwhile, another voice exists within us—it's a still small voice from somewhere deep within. It is actually the truth of who we are, and it is whispering and reminding—it is also relentless its pursuit to remind you that you are enough and that you matter. It is the voice of dreams and possibilities, of passions, visions and aspirations. It is the voice of certainty and it will return again and again for a lifetime; beckoning you to remember, encouraging you to take action and inviting you to believe in your strength and your purpose.

It's important that you know that once you make a decision to rise up and anchor in—to whatever vision you decide to create for your life, every excuse will be right there waiting for you. I'm not smart enough, I don't have enough money, I'm afraid, I don't know how, I'm too fat, I'm not good enough and I don't have what it takes. The list goes on and on and the voice of doubt, fear, rejection and unworthiness will go into overdrive to keep you right where you are.

I choose this day to draw a line in the sand—to make a vow, a solemn (from the soul) promise to never use my words as a weapon or an excuse. I remember to be mindful that whether it is my own inner voice or the words that I speak out loud—they are powerful and impactful. I will use my voice for good because I understand the hurt and pain I am inflicting on myself and others when I use my words as a weapon, and that is not the place I want to live from. Today I will pay close attention to how I show up for myself and for others.

I will not make excuses. I will be disciplined and courageous—I will remember that I am always learning and growing. I will take a stand for what is right. Today is a blessing, it is a new beginning. I take advantage of every opportunity to be kind and considerate and I will be thoughtful of the words I use.

Notes and Reflections

Courage

As you begin brand new this day....
Remember that you are enough.
Remember that you are filled with a Spirit of Love,
and that everything you need lies within you.
Remember that you are strong and courageous·
and that the stirring within you
is a reminder that you are growing.
Release every fear and ground in this truth,
knowing that you are on a journey of expansion·
Remember that growth is always on
the other side of fear,
and that Life is Always conspiring
for your greater good.
Stay true to your highest vision·
because your dreams are dynamically moving
into the reality of your life!

Sylvia Castillo

13. I don't partake in rumors and gossip, for I absolutely know that there is no power or personal growth in the depreciation of another

What a huge opportunity to self-check, how much time of my life's energy do I give to hear-say, fabrication and slander? More often than not gossip and rumors are about my need to tell "my story" or "my side" of a challenge or situation to another person so I can defend, justify, and basically get approval that I'm right. It's like I need someone to take my side so that I can feel OK about bashing and trash talking.

The tendency as a listener to participate in another person's drama happens for several reasons: because it makes you feel important that they chose you to share with, because it's easier to focus on someone else than to look at your own "stuff," or because there is something about the energy and production of the drama that is almost addictive. It creates an adrenaline rush or a high, kind of like a real-life Jerry Springer marathon.

Our insecurities perpetuate the drama of rumors and gossip. If you're willing to look closely and honestly at your own life and relationships, it's likely that there are issues closer than you think. Often times, when you have several close friends and you are the one that attracts different people, you probably have friends that don't necessarily like each other but tolerate each other because of their mutual friendship with you. What happens if you find yourself in a conversation with one friend who is trash talking the other friend? The way you handle this situation, and the perspective you have actually says a lot about the kind of person and friend you are in general.

As a neutral third party, when someone comes to you with a story that involves having to make a choice or pick a side, it does no good to choose a side without even having enough information to give constructive feedback. It would be so much more beneficial for everyone if we all adhered to the 24-hour rule. The premise is this: when something happens with someone that upsets or disturbs you for whatever reason, you have 24-hours to clear with that person. You don't seek advice, or council from a friend, you don't post on Facebook, or tweet your drama, you don't go looking for approval from any outside source. To "clear" means that you approach the person you have an issue with from a place of curiosity and the desire to understand, because here's the truth—whenever there is an issue typically it is because of a misunderstanding. When we take time to listen, clarify, and figure out where things went wrong, it offers the opportunity to create a new experience.

And what about those friends who have problems with each other but not with you? Do you stay neutral or do you play sides? What team are you on? True and lasting friendships dare to tell the truth. They do not compromise lies for the truth for fear of backlash, and they do not tolerate playing games or using people. If you are brave enough to face the truth, even when it is uncomfortable or even risks friendships, you will create an intimacy (into me I see) in a way that you may have never experienced.

Rumors and gossip really do keep us from being the absolute best version of ourselves that we can be. It is a test of our personal integrity and character to stay open and honest and to make being in alignment with ourselves more important than being seen or getting someone else approval. When we really get down to doing the work, we realize that the most important acceptance that we could ever hope to have, is the acceptance of ourselves.

So, the 24-hour rule starts now. Who this week will you clear with? How will you approach this from a place of opportunity and possibility? What amends need to be made?

Notes and Reflections

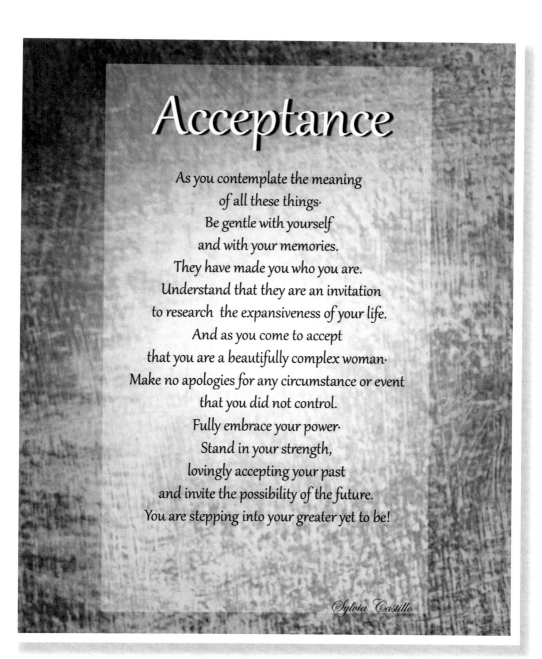

Acceptance

As you contemplate the meaning
of all these things.
Be gentle with yourself
and with your memories.
They have made you who you are.
Understand that they are an invitation
to research the expansiveness of your life.
And as you come to accept
that you are a beautifully complex woman.
Make no apologies for any circumstance or event
that you did not control.
Fully embrace your power.
Stand in your strength,
lovingly accepting your past
and invite the possibility of the future.
You are stepping into your greater yet to be!

Sylvia Castillo

14. I don't take things personally

This is the second agreement in the four that we will be exploring. Let's be real—we take just about everything personally. Have you ever walked into a room and thought that the conversation was about you? Immediately there is a feeling of upset and frustration, an entire story made up. You might have even thought about what was being said and then spent time thinking about how you would respond. In a matter of a few minutes, an entire situation erupted. You even decided how you would get your revenge. Your face was flushed, your heartbeat rose, and just thinking about it made things worse. And the crazy thing is: it never even actually happened! It was all made up—a story in your mind that went left field, and you went with it, blood pressure and all.

Maybe you've heard someone receive a compliment, and you wondered why you didn't get one. The mind immediately searching for the why. Maybe I'm not good enough, maybe they really don't like and appreciate me like I thought? In an instant, another made up story. No facts, no reason, not even a conversation. Just a story, completely made up, wreaking havoc in your mind and generating toxins in your body.

Can you even imagine how often your feelings get hurt and no one besides you even knows? We take it all personally, we think someone else's drama is really about us, we think because they are upset, and we must have done something wrong. Someone has an attitude and right away we're there to defend and destroy or walk out. How about the made-up story when someone gives you a look?! How dare she look at me like that, she's a ….

Right?! It's true. We've all done it at some time or another.

The interesting thing is this: we see through our own filter, and no one else is responsible for the way we interpret life. If we imagine that everyone is out to get us, they are—**and** we will even find the evidence to prove it right because it is done unto us "As We Believe."

Did you ever find out the truth about their conversation? They weren't talking about you: one of them was actually looking for some advice about a challenge and the other was listening to her story. The way the other one looked at you: she had never seen such beautiful hair and was wondering to herself if it was time for a new updated look. You were actually in that moment inspiration for someone else, but couldn't see it because your vision was blurred by your own BS.

Our inner dialogue has been programmed by the voice of our past. By our experiences—good or bad, right or wrong. When we begin to explore our innermost thoughts, when we are finally tired of blaming everyone else for our conditions and when we are ready for growth and expansion, we will begin the most important work of our lives: the inner exploration. There is no deeper or more profound journey than that of going within—into the closet of our mind, and it is here that we will pierce the veil of illusion. Everyone is off the hook, even the ones who hurt us.

We will decide to purify our minds and our vision, to see the best in everyone, even when someone else cannot see it for themselves. We will not take things personally. We will become witnesses to our self-talk—not to judge in any way, but to be curiously investigating the voices that are at play in our minds.

Begin a practice: I commit this week to not taking things personally, and I practice patience and compassion with myself and others when I see, hear or experience anything that would have me be anything other than the very best version of myself. Today, I know that everything is ultimately for my highest good and I choose to be kind and loving as much as I possibly can.

Notes and Reflections

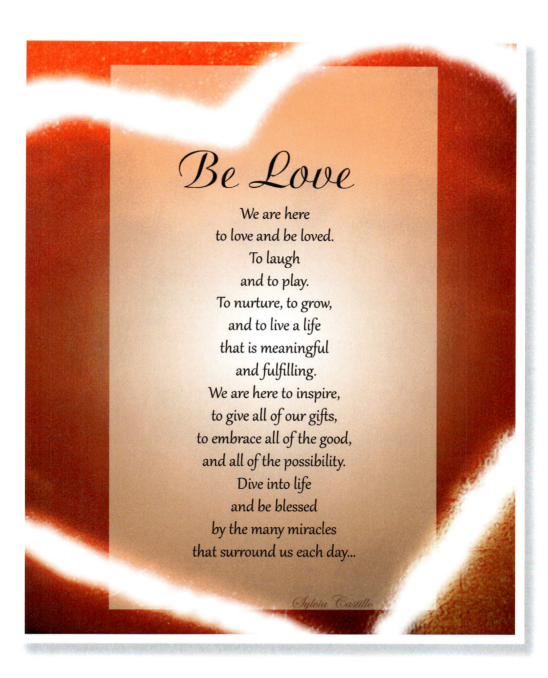

Be Love

We are here
to love and be loved.
To laugh
and to play.
To nurture, to grow,
and to live a life
that is meaningful
and fulfilling.
We are here to inspire,
to give all of our gifts,
to embrace all of the good,
and all of the possibility.
Dive into life
and be blessed
by the many miracles
that surround us each day...

Sylvia Castillo

15. I recognize that we are all on a journey—learning, growing, discovering, finding, reaching and figuring out our own plan

We really are on a journey. It's a journey of self-discovery. It's a beautiful story of accepting and loving ourselves beyond all appearances, mistakes, and regrets.

We are all individually and collectively learning, growing, discovering, finding, reaching, and figuring out our own plan.

It's true. We are all in various places on our life's journey, and as much as it would be wise to stay on the path of growth, we are human. We remember and forget, we hide and get found, we hurt and heal, we love ourselves and we self-sabotage, we judge and are joyful, we celebrate and condemn, we feast and then experience famine, we know pleasure and pain, love, and loss and everything else in between.

There is no right or wrong in the way of contrast; in other words, how can we measure pleasure without knowing pain? If I am a fish in water, I don't know the depth, the clarity, the importance, and the feeling of water until I am without it, *and* it is only in the absence or in the contrast that I can even clarify my desire to be and stay in the water.

This simple yet profound explanation could be the elixir of love and understanding that would heal all wounds, unite enemies, build bridges, and cultivate faith. It would give new meaning to seek understanding beyond all appearances.

Do you remember the prodigal son? How he got lost and spent all he had? He longed not only for food, but to go back home to shelter, safety, and the love of family.

Have you ever gotten lost? Have you ever made an error in your judgment or in your behavior that hurt someone in a way that you didn't even know you were capable of?

Have you ever needed to ask for forgiveness? Have you ever learned from your mistake, or decided to draw a line in the sand for what you stood for because maybe there were times in your life that you didn't stand for anything?

So, the son went home; head down, ashamed, embarrassed, feeling completely unworthy, not knowing what would happen when he went back—he confessed his errors in judgment, and his father looked at him with such compassion and immediately forgave him. Not only was the son forgiven, he was celebrated with an enormous feast. His father recognized that his son who once was dead was now found.

The lesson is profound—and possibly more profound to those who have genuinely felt sorrow and remorse for actions that caused another harm. To those who have been embarrassed and ashamed, whose pain was beyond regretful, for those who may have wanted to die in the face of their mistake, this forgiveness is a resurrection. Forgiveness will literally give new life to the one who suffers internally.

There is no way to measure the enormity of this kind of forgiveness. It is beyond understanding, beyond our human comprehension. There is something about the depth of love when you truly forgive, and The gift of forgiveness opens the heart of the giver in ways that will alter the path of life forever.

We are all on a journey, learning growing, discovering, finding, reaching, and figuring out our own plan. So say to yourself: Today, I consciously bring love and compassion into my life because it changes everything.

Notes and Reflections

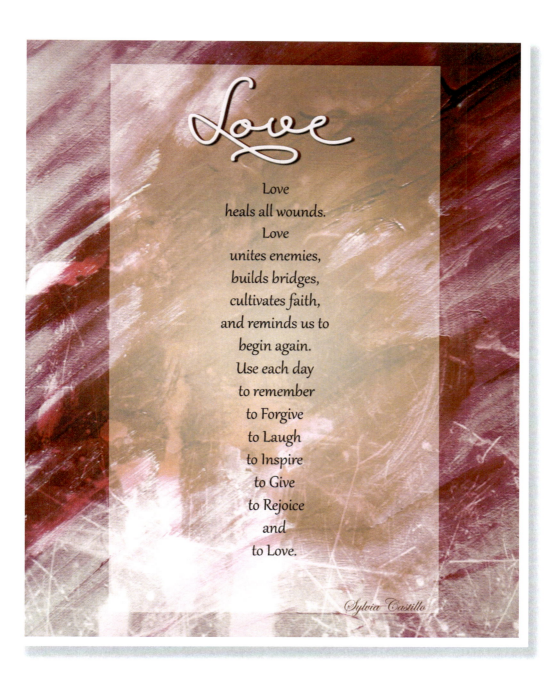

Love

Love
heals all wounds.
Love
unites enemies,
builds bridges,
cultivates faith,
and reminds us to
begin again.
Use each day
to remember
to Forgive
to Laugh
to Inspire
to Give
to Rejoice
and
to Love.

Sylvia Castillo

16. When I stay committed to my highest vision, when I am in integrity with myself, I approach others with patience and humility

When I stay committed to my highest vision, this in itself is such an important sentence. Before I can be committed to my highest vision, I must first have a vision. When this journey started fifteen weeks ago, creating a vision for our lives was one of the first steps. Having a vision that is written down is so important. It helps to provide clarity. Writing it down and spelling it out gives us the opportunity to work backwards to create a roadmap with milestones and benchmarks—indicators that we are on the right track.

It is said that where there is no vision, the people will perish. Having a vision gives us something to work toward. It is where we focus on our passion and our purpose and where we get to decide and declare for ourselves what is possible.

If you have a vision written down, congratulations! If you still need to get your vision from your head onto paper, return to week 4 to write down your vision.

The interesting thing is this: when we have a vision, when we are working towards something big or something we are excited about, we don't have the drama. We're too busy getting things done. We're excited about the possibilities, we're on fire following our deepest desires and moving forward feels good. If your life is in chaos and you feel a lack of direction and purpose, it is likely that you don't have a vision and/or goals that you are working on and chances are that you may be suffering internally. This is not to say that life doesn't happen or that things are perfect when you have a vision; however, there is a gap between people who have ambitions and aspirations that they are following and those who do not.

When I am in integrity with myself, I listen to the still small voice within—the one that is reminding me that I am strong, powerful, and worthy. When I am in integrity with myself, I don't need to pretend to be someone I'm not. I love and accept myself, I decide what virtues and morals I stand for and what I am willing to stand up for, I set boundaries and standards for myself and for my life and use them to guide me—and, I draw a line in the sand to those people, places, or things that are not in alignment with my highest vision.

These seemingly insignificant choices in our lives are actually monumental. The results and experiences we have in our lives will be in direct proportion to the vision or lack of vision we have in our lives.

When we know and understand this message and these ideas to be truth, we do approach others with patience and humility. "Forgive them father for they do not know." Instead of making judgments or throwing stones at others for where they have been or what they have done, we choose to be curious, to learn more about where another has been, and we listen with the desire to understand.

For those who are ready to grow, they will hear and recognize these words will be inspiring, and they will offer hope and possibility. For the one that is ready to go within, to look for answers from the inside out—for the one who starts with gratitude and finishes with grace and humility—much is guaranteed.

Look at yourself and say: Today, I recommit to my highest vision. I start right where I am, releasing all judgments and comparisons. I attune myself to the highest vision and possibility for my life, and I consciously make decisions and choices that support my goals to ensure that I am on a path of growth. I am patient with myself and others, and I remember that life is always conspiring for my greater good.

Notes and Reflections

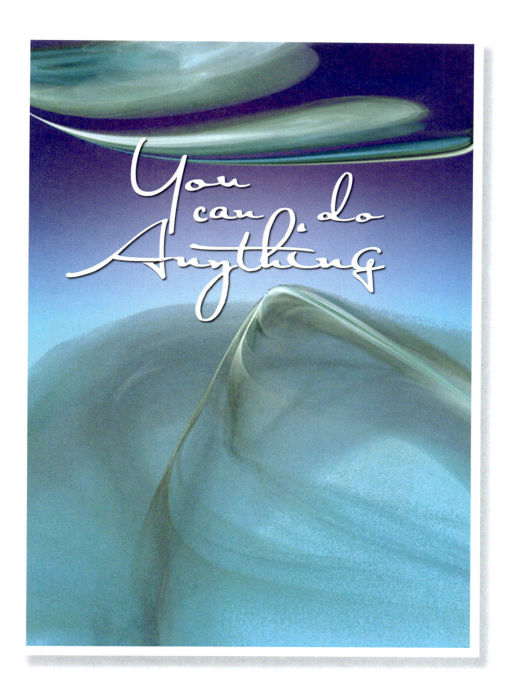

17. I know that each of us is doing the best we can with our current level of awareness— and I honor that space

When we truly come to understand this statement, our perception shifts. We begin interpreting people and events from a place of curiosity and the desire to understand.

We don't take things personally because we really get that people operate from *their* place of awareness, and most of the time, it has nothing to do with us. When I honor, which means to have respect in one's beliefs and actions, I let others be who and where they are without it causing an interruption for me.

So consider this: Where is life calling for you to grow and focus on your own level of awareness. How might you stand in your own power? What does life have to offer without drama and chaos? What might be possible if your attention was focused on your goals, vision, growth, and expansion?

They say that birds of a feather flock together and your tribe sets your vibe. Does your tribe lift you up? Do they hold you accountable and call you out on your BS? If your tribe is not inspiring you to be the best you can be, you might want to consider taking an inventory. Seriously, if you are not engaging with people that motivate and encourage you to be more, do more, and have more, it may be time to take an inventory.

We can honor the space of all people and at the same time make a conscious choice to not operate or spend our life's energy on people and circumstances that do not support our highest vision. Where we are and how we *feel* is critical to our expansion.

The opportunity that each of us have when we go within and seek strength from the inside out is that we don't rely on external situations to define how we will show up in our own lives. We call on a place within that knows only strength, love, and possibility—and we lean into this truth to seek greater and greater understanding.

There's a game that people play when they are "people watching." They make up stories about who other people are because of how they are dressed and what they look like. Sometimes the stories are incredibly detailed; it's like you already know everything. There is a pre-judgement and an acceptance or denial made in a matter of seconds.

It's always good to remember that people are products of their environment, a collection of the stories they made up, experiencing the results they created. It's not a bad idea to have a little more gratitude and compassion wherever they and we might be.

> *"If we could read the history of our friends and enemies, we would find in each man/woman's life enough sorrow and suffering to disarm all hostility."*
> *~ Henry Wadsworth Longfellow*

Decide to be the witness and leave the judge and jury to the universe to work out whatever karma or consequence is needed as it relates to others. Just notice where you spend your time and with who; wherever you are, be honest with yourself and just notice if you are on the path of your vision, you'll know it in your heart. Your internal guidance system will never leave you. Take time this week to honor the part of you that is ready to grow and become. It's what we're here to do.

Notes and Reflections

SENDING YOU LOTS OF LOVE AS YOU EMBRACE YOUR TRUTH

Here we are at a crossroads. I long for time to stand still, that I might somehow be able to go back. Wishing I could unwind time – that I might be able to seek out what it was or where it began to turn.

I have fought and struggled, attempting to control the circumstances and change the outcome, and in my anger and frustration I have said things that I wish I could take back.

My heart aches for you to see what I see – the truth about you. That you are strong and powerful, that you have such amazing potential. And I'm lost in the struggle because I recognize that my resistance is futile.

I see now that it is pointless for me to resist what is – not that I don't believe in you, the truth is that I only want the best for you.

I have come to accept that this is what you have to know for yourself – it is your journey and you are the only person that can heal your perception. There is no pill, no ticket, no escape, excuses and no answer outside of yourself, and as long as you keep looking "out there" you will be lost. Forever searching for something that doesn't exist.

The answers are within you. Waiting for you to rise up, beckoning you to listen to the still small voice within. And it will wait, and wait, and wait…

You see we are all at choice, given the absolute freedom to do what we choose. Dominion over our thoughts and actions. Full responsibility, right where we are.

So I will stand here – grounded in the truth, hoping that you come to see your own beauty, praying you will heal the wounds within you - trusting you will come through your personal battle without a war. And knowing that eventually you will come to love and accept yourself.

I will stand here, holding space for you, knowing your truth, believing in you and loving you right where you are...

~Sylvia Castillo

18. I release all demands and expectations that keep me in judgment

The work of personal development is a constant opportunity for self-reflection. It is a journey of continuous evolution, and one that allows each of us to simply be the witness and leave the judge and jury to a higher power. Expectations of others are the cause of so much disappointment and frustration, especially when the expectation requires someone else to be responsible for your joy and happiness. And what about the demands others place on us? The insistent request as if made by right—by the righteous. The question then becomes am I the witness or the judge and jury?

What do you do with judgement when you can feel it coming from another? Do you get defensive or angry? or do you get combative and aggressive? Do you shrink and disappear or fight back? All of these are responses that some would call completely justifiable; however when you get to a place where you can see that the one judging is the one to have compassion for, it changes everything.

There was a lady whose son was in constant trouble. She tried to teach him right from wrong and good from bad, although somehow he always had a way to find trouble and he always placed the blame outside of himself. They did this, or they did that—he unfortunately never took responsibility for his actions. The lady was depressed, she was mortified that her son continued to make unhealthy choices, and she felt responsible for actions. Now that he had added drugs to his list of bad habits, she was at her wits end, and it was killing her—literally. She was getting sick to the point of risking her own health, much of it caused by self-doubt, self-judgment, and huge disappointment.

From the outside looking in, these two were a hot mess. There was judgment and condemnation added to an expectation that the lady should have forced her son to make better choices. The judge and jury were out building their case, and it looked as though it would be a life sentence and a self-fulfilling prophecy of cyclical abuse.

The witness, however, took a different perspective. The witness chose to have a heart and eyes of compassion. The witness wondered what the boy was running from and realized that the boy was suffering from a masculine wound. It's the kind of wound that is created in a boy's informative years. It's the kind of wound that is created from a message from another man that you don't measure up and you're not good enough. It's the kind of wound that one attempts to fill with pleasure because the pain is so deep. And once a boy begins the process of numbing the pain with drugs, the road is almost always devastation.

The witness knew that there was only one solution for the healing of a masculine wound and encouraged the lady and young man to seek answers at the "The Table." You see, the founder of "The Table" understood that only masculine energy could heal a masculine wound, and try as she might his mother could cry, plead, and beg for change and change would never come.

The boy, now a young man, took a seat at "The Table." He learned about a power that resided in him. He learned about the way of the warrior, the importance of standing with men of purpose, and little by little his healing had begun. You see condemnation by the judge and jury is never the solution. It is the unconditional love of the father, our father who heals all things. Our opportunity every day is to cooperate with the power of love, to let it inform our thoughts, impress upon our actions, and to wash over every place of unworthiness.

Today, I resolve to see with eyes of compassion for myself and others. To be the witness and to draw a line in the sand for all the ways that I will show up in honesty and integrity. Today, I resolve to be the leader that others would follow because I lead with integrity, purpose and ONEness.

Notes and Reflections

19. and I forgive myself and others for our misgivings

Forgiveness is the process of purification. It is a line in the sand, a fresh start, a conscious choice and another chance to being again. Forgiveness and love are the perfect elixir to heal all things—betrayal, condemnation, neglect, wrongdoing, jealousy, hate, judgement, prejudice, adultery, violence, and war.

The process of forgiveness, however, is not to be taken lightly. When we draw a line in the sand, take a stand, or commit to a new way of showing up, we must do it or suffer the natural consequences of cause and effect.

We cannot expect to have or create positive outcomes if we are mired in behaviors, circumstances, or situations that are not fair and just and of honesty and integrity. One way that we can really identify this for ourselves is to notice if we are the same person everywhere we go. If there are certain behaviors that some people do not see, habits and language that are kept hidden or things that are discussed or expressed that cannot be shared openly, there is probably an opportunity to get clear about who you are and what you stand for.

Forgiveness of self requires that a new behavior be embraced. True forgiveness sees inward at the hurt caused to another and commits to a new way of being. There is no tricking the soul. One cannot move out of unforgiveness while still causing harm to others.

Acceptance and forgiveness of another can offer freedom from pain, liberation from toxic energy that is constantly attacking, and it can also offer what to some is considered: The Third Way. It is the unknowable path that can only be discovered through the forgiveness process.

This is perhaps the most significant part of my own personal journey. To be the one to ask for forgiveness.

I cannot begin to tell you the pain that I inflicted on my husband, my family, and myself. I did the unthinkable. I betrayed our vows. I had an affair. I honestly don't know how we managed to keep it together. I will not make excuses or ask anyone to understand. There is no way to articulate the the depth of pain that each of us experienced because of my actions.

I talk a lot about how we create our own reality and the damage that followed my actions were undeniable. What I personally experienced as a result of my infidelity was deep inconsolable pain and a series of events that were a direct result of where I had placed my attention. I wanted to end my life. There was no way that I could make sense of who I claimed to be in the world with my actions.

I can tell you that forgiveness is an amazing gift. I can say without a doubt that the reason that we are still together is because my husband extended forgiveness to me. I will never forget the way he looked at me. It was over a year later. We were having a deep and emotional conversation. He looked at me with such love and compassion and said that he had already forgiven me and that I needed to forgive myself.

I would never wish these events on anyone, and yet, I don't know if in my lifetime I would understand the significance of forgiveness in the way that I do now.

Forgiveness and unconditional love saves lives. It is so much more than something you do for yourself to release another. It is an elixir that carries with it the power to heal in ways we could never know. It is a profound and selfless extension of love that is alchemy in its truest form.

No one could have imagined all of the good or have foreseen all the possibility of what some may have considered unforgivable. The Third Way—the way of unforeseen possibility, of forgiveness—offers ideas, passions, and possibilities that are sourced from the Spirit. They are unknowable and cannot be figured out in the mind. It is the work of the heart, the elixir of love, and the power of Spirit that only know. Our opportunity is to trust, to have faith, and to forgive.

Where will you find the opportunity to look for The Third Way? Where is there an opportunity to create a new story? Are there areas of your life where you cannot forgive, and yet other areas where you would hope that you might be forgiven? We cannot ask for something we are not willing to give. Our reasons and justifications will be the first thing that we will need to reconcile and release before we will experience true peace.

forgiveness

Looking back, I recognize it was all for me.
Every circumstance, every situation,
and every perceived obstacle.
leading me to this moment.
I have come to realize
that everything happens for
my highest good,
and in this awakening, I remember
the depth of the many gifts and lessons.
I am not scared and broken.
I am not separate or invaluable.
I am strong and powerful.
I am humbled and willing.
I am courageous,
I am worthy,
and I am ready to live.

Sylvia Castillo

20. I don't assume anything

What does life look like when we don't assume anything? We don't make up stories about what things mean. My communication is impeccable, or at least I'm making an effort and that I seek first to understand rather than to role play things out in my mind. How often do we do that?

We're feeling good about life and our relationships. Then, someone behaves in a certain way, and we take it to the worst case scenario. We think about it so much that we elaborate on every horrible detail and gather evidence of the past to support a point of view and thought process that is entirely made up. We go into fight mode, and we bring a negative energy to the other person and begin to create a reality that matches our negativity. We can even go so far as to single ourselves out—to think that we don't matter and that we don't belong; meanwhile, others have no clue what is going on inside because we "play the role." We act as though everything is ok when in fact we feel anger, depression, anxiety, jealously, and pain all the while showing a smile. We assume we don't matter, that we're not enough, that we don't belong, and that what we have to contribute means nothing when that's not the truth at all. What does life look like when we're not assuming the worst?

What if I were able to keep one eye on the inside and just notice where I am in my body—interestingly enough when we decide to be led by the heart and not our minds our perspective begins to shift. I am able to let someone else be who they are and allow them to have their experience without thinking it has anything to do with me. How do we begin to change a pattern, a thought process and behavior that has been running on auto-pilot our whole lives?

It's about tuning in, about making a conscious choice to pay attention to where we are operating from. Ask yourself: Am I in my head making things up? Do I have all of the facts? Am I willing to see the situation from another perspective? We have an amazing amount of freedom to choose how we will see our world and what we will make of our stories—and interestingly enough, our stories will set the stage for all that we experience in our life.

What if we made a decision to consciously pay attention to the times when we are angry, upset, and assuming? What if we took a moment to stop, breathe, and ground from a different place? What if our perspective was creating our reality and all we had to do was change the way we looked at our circumstances and situations? We've been running on autopilot for a long time, thinking that "it's just the way things are" when in fact it's the way it is because we are 100% responsible for our relationships and our results, and if we are not satisfied with our current state of affairs, the only place that we can go that will have a lasting effect is within.

Today's Practice: I start with me. I commit to notice how I am reacting, responding, and showing up in general. I will pay attention to the voices in my head and notice if it is a voice of acceptance, love, and possibility or if it is one of judgement, fear, and contradiction. Today, I choose not to assume anything.

Notes and Reflections

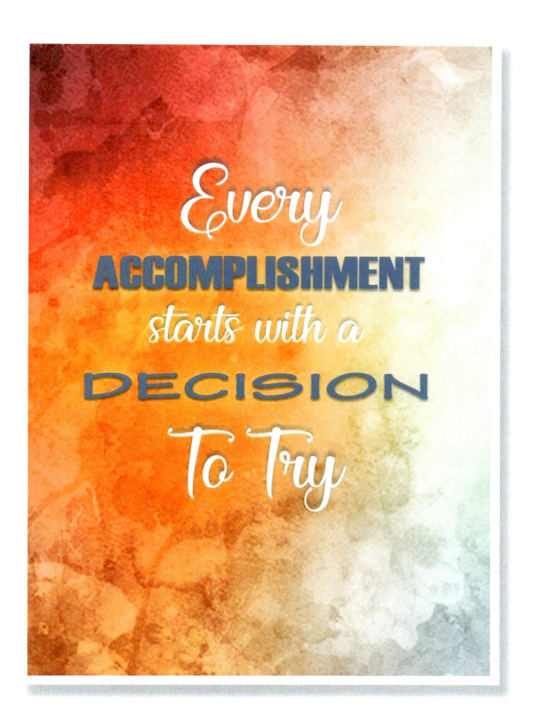

21. I accept full and total responsibility for my life

What does that even mean to accept full and total responsibility for my life? First of all, it means that everybody is off the hook. Parents that were physically or emotionally disconnected or unavailable, a neighbor who may have said or done things that violated you and your space, a wife who cheated, a husband who stole, a boyfriend that was a batterer, a best friend who lied, an acquaintance who was slanderous, kids that were disrespectful, deceitful, or drug-induced—the list goes on and on as it always has and probably always will. Maybe you were the perpetrator and it was you who did the violating. Either way, it's in the past.

Everyone is off the hook. No one is responsible for my success or failure, and I consciously choose today to take responsibility for my life. No more excuses, no more should have's, no more looking back at the past or defining myself or my future from events that may or may not have been out of my control. No more operating from a place of fear, scarcity, lack, regret, or shame.

Today I accept full and total responsibility for my life and that means I will draw a line the sand, and this line in the sand is not to be taken lightly. It is not a joke or a game. Seriously, we cannot be the violator or the victim and be ready to create new and different results in our lives. It just doesn't work that way.

It's time to ask different questions: Instead of, "Why me? Why did this happen? How can I get over this?" it's time to change the dialogue. The questions to ask are: What is alive in me? What is wanting to be birthed? Where can I show up and make a difference? How is my life attempting to show me that it's time for change?

What are you willing to give up, stop doing or forgive so that you can release the chains of your own bondage? We all know the saying that insanity is doing the same thing over and over and expecting different results and yet what are you doing different?

Proclaim today that: I will not focus on things I could not or would not control and I pay close attention to the desires of my heart. Ask: What is calling me? What do I miss doing? Where am I ready to grow, expand and discover? Affirm: It is only in this exploration of my inner self that I can begin to move away from patterns, behaviors and a protective personality that wants to keep me in the same little box that I've always been in.

The garden is an amazing analogy for the results in our lives. If you've ever planted a garden, you know that a tomato seed will not produce corn. The seeds of our negative thoughts and words will not produce positive results. Once seeds are planted, we must also tend to the garden with nutrients; sunlight, water, and maybe even Miracle Grow. And we must tend on a daily basis or the weeds will choke the life right out of the garden. We must also be patient, because the day you plant the seed is not the day you eat the fruit. So, what in your life is representative of the weeds, and who or what must be removed? Maybe the soil of your life's garden needs to be completely tilled and turned over so that something new might grow. You cannot put poison in, on or around your garden and expect to have a healthy, vibrant, and producing harvest. It is insanity.

Proclaim, I will draw a line in the sand and I will not feel fearful, anxious, or afraid. I choose this day to let go of thought processes, patterns, and people that don't align with the highest vision for my life. Today, I am nurturing the garden of my life and, I am committed to producing positive results because I am taking full and total responsibility for my life.

Notes and Reflections

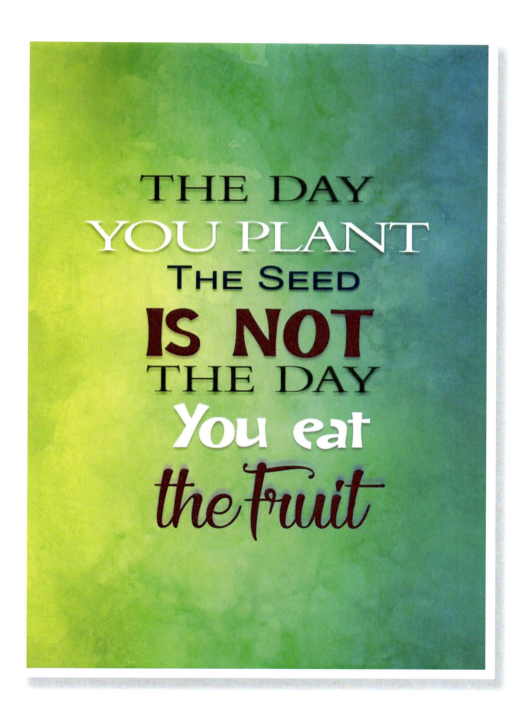

22. for my relationships, I accept full and total responsibility

Relationships give us the perfect opportunity for learning so much about ourselves, if we are willing to authentically explore this area of our lives and ourselves we will come to learn where we are weak and vulnerable, where we are overbearing and impulsive, where we are loving and nurturing, where we withhold, and where we are generous. An intimate relationship that has a foundation of trust and respect and one that is honest and real will be one of the greatest experiences we will ever have.

Rest assured that we will feel every emotion in our relationships, the highs and the lows, right and wrong, the good, the bad, and the ugly—the full spectrum. The gift of a relationship that can withstand the full experience of obstacles, adversity, challenge, and forgiveness is an intimacy with a depth of love that not everyone experiences.

You see, we are so quick to call the game. So quick to judge and think that everything must look a particular way. Some think that it's all black and white, and the truth is that it's not really anything until we add our story to it, until we name it, judge it or give meaning to it. Our perspective, our outlook, and our thought process will determine how deep we can love, how easily we can accept, how often we will be vulnerable, and how much of an impact we will have in our own lives and in the lives of others. If our perspective is old and outdated, if it belongs to someone else, or if we are on autopilot most of our lives, it's almost certain that we will have a victim perspective and feel like life is happening to us and that we don't have much or any control of the circumstances of our lives.

The flip side of that is 100% responsibility. Proclaim: I will choose to look within. I will pay attention to the things, people, and words that "trigger" me because I understand that this is where my own healing will take place. There is no crystal ball, magic pill or prescription that will do the work for me. In fact, it's a life-long process of letting go. Letting go of the idea that someone else is responsible for my happiness or success, letting go of the idea that that relationships must look a certain way, letting go of the idea that he or she must act or be a certain way in order for me to be ok.

In this process of going inward, we do need to recognize that birds of a feather flock together and that not everyone is equally yoked; in other words, we are all in different levels of understanding, experience, and results—and if I am ready to reach new heights in my personal and professional relationships, I must be willing to take an inventory of those who are currently in my life. Who are the ones that lift me up and see me bigger than I see myself? Who is holding me accountable? Who doesn't accept my excuses and calls me on my BS? Who are those who make excuses for me? Who encourage me in the opposite direction of my dreams and desires. Not good, bad, right or wrong—just an inventory.

Here's even more to consider: It is one thing to be oblivious to it, and it is another to take 100% responsibility and to consciously choose who I will surround myself with. And what about the relationship I have with myself? Where am I arguing for my own limitations? Where in my life am I getting out of the box and being uncomfortable? Growth and expansion does not happen in our comfort zone.

And now, I affirm: Today, I choose to take an inventory of my relationships. How will I express my love and gratitude to those I want to have a closer relationship with? Who will be my fox hole buddy and hold me accountable? What will I do for myself; for my own health and wellbeing? Where will I contribute and how will I make a difference? I am committed to creating happy, healthy and harmonious relationships in my life. I will focus on being the very best version of me and allow grace to bring new and supportive relationships into my life.

Notes and Reflections

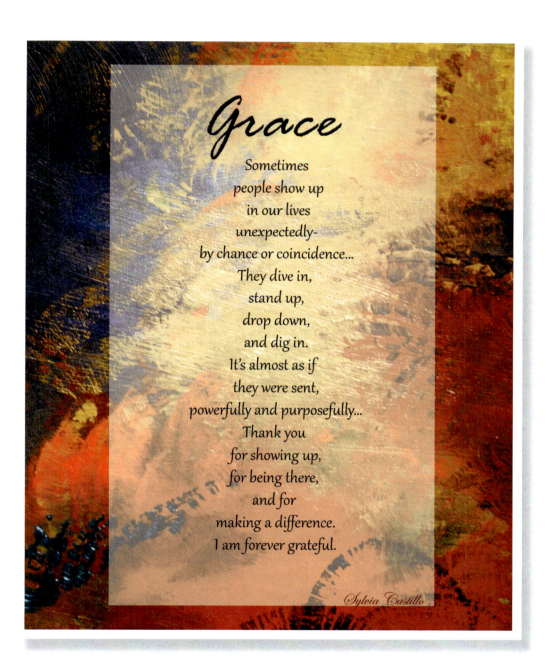

Grace

Sometimes
people show up
in our lives
unexpectedly-
by chance or coincidence...
They dive in,
stand up,
drop down,
and dig in.
It's almost as if
they were sent,
powerfully and purposefully...
Thank you
for showing up,
for being there,
and for
making a difference.
I am forever grateful.

Sylvia Castillo

23. and for my results, I accept full and total responsibility

What does the sum total of my life look like? What things am I proud of? Where am I devoted and making a difference? Where do I give my time and energy? How is my health and well-being? How's my work and personal contribution? How are my relationships with others and myself? Am I showing up authentically? Is my life's path the one I want to be on? Am I inspired or inspiring? Am I leaving a legacy I would be proud of?

If I am to accept full and total responsibility for my results, it would be a good idea to take a look at the entire picture, the full scope and sum total of my results—an inventory of everything.

This is not about blame, shame, or guilt. It's about taking an honest look at where things are on track and where there is room for improvement—or maybe a complete overhaul. In the very beginning of this journey, we talked about a vision for your life. Some people refer to it as a blueprint, a compass or a life map. Did you create one for yourself? Are you moving in the direction of something that you can measure? Or are you just moving in a circle with no particular goal, destination or end result in mind?

Most of those who have achieved a desired level of success have the same consistent message about writing down our goals and vision. It's basically a requirement; it's important to have an intention so that we know where to give our attention. Without it, we're on an undirected journey. The opportunity is to be a deliberate creator—to choose, create, explore, discover, and experience the ideas and dreams that live in our core. When we give our attention to this possibility and expansion, to excitement and enthusiastic anticipation, and we operate from an energy of positivity.

The flip side of that is fear; it's being so caught up the ego or protective personality that the voice of unworthiness and not good enoughness keep us from doing anything outside of our comfort level.

Remember the seed? What we plant grows; the tomato seed is not coming up corn or daisies. We don't know how it happens, but we trust the soil which is the creative medium that makes its growth possible. We know that if we dig up the seed before it has a chance to do what it does, we ruin the process. While we are patiently waiting—well some not so patiently—it doesn't make the process any faster by worrying. We must also tend to the garden: sharpening tools, tilling, watering, fertilizing, pruning, protecting, and managing the overall needs of the garden. And what happens if we stop midway? The weeds are certain to choke out the life of the garden. We don't know why: it's just the way it works and if having a healthy harvest is important to us, we will have to tend to it daily.

The same is true for us. Ask yourself: are your dreams and desires full and ripe with experiences and results the way you intended? What does daily tending look like? What must you be doing on a daily basis and who must you become to create it? *Your Life Is* the garden. How is your harvest? Is it what you want? Are you willing to cultivate your mindset, water your dreams, fertilize your income, protect your space, nurture your spirituality, and tend to your health and well-being? Who or what represents the weeds in your life that need to be removed? You are the gardener and the harvest is your life. Your thoughts, words, and actions are the seeds you are planting, and everything that you put into it will become the fruits of your life. What you reap you sow and what you plant will grow.

Affirm: Today, I recommit myself to my results; I speak my truth and plant seeds of possibility.

Notes and Reflections

24. If there is something I need to know, I ask

How often do you need help and don't ask for it? How many times would it have been helpful to have support, but instead you made up a story about why you couldn't or shouldn't ask for it? Maybe you're thinking: They're too busy, or I'm not on their list of "important" people. So, you don't ask, you don't know and right within that decision we are back to assuming. Creating stories, toxins and worst case sinearo.

If you are asking for support, be sure that you give details and communicate effectively. If you need something done in a certain amount of time, that is critical information. We are setting ourselves up for disappointment and failure if we don't ask for exactly what we need—timeline and all. When we get upset at someone for letting us down, we must also be willing to look at the way that we communicated—or the lack of communication which led to our disappointment.

The other side of this coin is that you might be the one being asked, and you are not communicating honestly and authentically. This game can go on for a lifetime. It's detrimental in relationships. Don't ask, don't tell. Sweep it all under the rug, let's not focus on anything that is important. We will give all of our time to fun and recreation, spin and tumble in the drama of things, and never get to greatness.

Each one of us has an opportunity to respond instead of react, to listen instead of assume, and to ask and be real about our answers. Imagine if every time you withheld the truth, an incurable scar appeared on your skin where it was visible to all. Imagine a lifetime of lies, secrets, half-truths, and hidden agendas. You would literally be untouchable—so filled with wounds that you would need to find something to numb the pain. Now the interesting thing is this: those wounds are real, they may not be visible for all to see, but you know the truth. Another hit on the pipe, another drink, another pill, another man or woman in your bed, and on and on and on.

There is a world of support, encouragement, love, harmony, and acceptance, and the question is: what world are you living in?

We are almost halfway through the journey of *My Agreements with Me*. Your vision is written out, you've created an inventory of your life and your relationships. Now, what does real support look like? Who is your foxhole buddy? Who is holding you accountable? Find a mentor, ask for help, be vulnerable. What will you create? Be accountable to yourself and ask for help.

We are all busy, and people still have time, and if they don't—move on. We get one chance in this physical body in this lifetime to be deliberate creators. We can stand back on the sidelines hoping someone notices the struggle, or you can put yourself out there in a way that is unique, special, vulnerable, and authentically you.

There is no need to apologize or ask for forgiveness or permission. You have done the work, and if you are honest with yourself you have drawn a line in the sand because you understand the necessity and the blessing of being in integrity all of the time.

They say, "Ask and it is given" and "Where there is no vision, the people will perish." You have a vision and you are asking. Don't sell yourself short and don't expect people to read between the lines. Ask for what you need and stay committed to this path of growth.

Affirm to yourself: I will be clear in asking for what I need. I invite support, collaboration, new friendships, and positive influences into my life.

Notes and Reflections

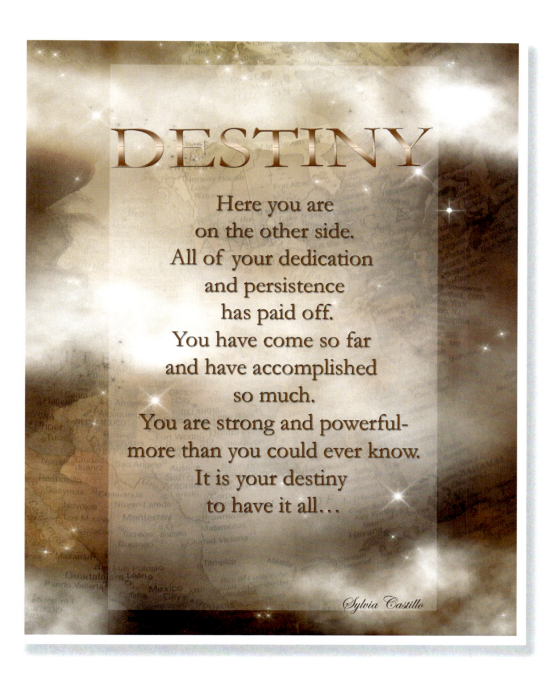

DESTINY

Here you are
on the other side.
All of your dedication
and persistence
has paid off.
You have come so far
and have accomplished
so much.
You are strong and powerful—
more than you could ever know.
It is your destiny
to have it all…

Sylvia Castillo

25. If there is something I need to say, I communicate

Communication is more than key; It's everything. Not just what we say but how we say it. How we emphasize a word, add a gesture or a look. It can completely alter the meaning of our words and the way that we show up with another person. Add to the mix assumptions, stories, parts left out, accusations, judgments, and feelings. What we intend or hope to say, how we articulate it, and the motive behind our words can be the difference between someone feeling heard or not, supported or not, loved or not.

We often withhold because we are in fear of the consequences of our communication. How often do we just not talk at all about what is really going on? How much time is spent hiding out? And how much of life is kept on the surface? Sports, weather, news, politics and clothes, nails and other people?

We have an opportunity every day to authentically express what we are thinking and feeling. It is our own personal responsibility to make sure that what we are expressing outwardly matches how we are feeling internally. Saying "yes" to something or someone while we are feeling overcommitted and resentful internally is a toxic combination. It creates anxiety and inner conflict. How can we communicate in such a way that allows us to say what we need to say while still honoring and respecting another and ourselves? If most of our communication is spent arguing, defending, and exploding we miss the opportunity to collaborate, create and support.

What we will find is that we are either operating in harmony or resistance, and this is true in our communication and in our lives in general. If what I want is open, honest, and authentic communication

I must be willing to give and lead with that in myself. (For the record, being open and honest doesn't give us permission to be rude, sarcastic, and disrespectful.)

In week 20, we looked at making assumptions and how detrimental they are to our relationships. As we continue to work on our communication, the invitation is to continue to notice when we shut down, when we get tense or closed off. What is it that is said or done that "triggers" us to react, feel defensive, and lash out? These are all places of exploration and healing within ourselves. As we keep one eye on the inside, we will begin to notice patterns, triggers, and a conversation with our self that tends to be the perspective we see, speak and live from. The question is: Does this serve me?

Where are we operating from most of the time? Is it our head or our hearts? Pay attention to the closest relationship you have—the one with yourself and/or a significant and meaningful relationship (regardless of who it is). In most cases, this is a person who you cherish, admire, and respect, and interestingly enough in a moment all of that can shift. We will literally say and do things to this person that are in complete contradiction to how we say we feel about them. In a state of negative headspace, we can often do say and do things that we would never think of saying or doing when we are grounded in our hearts.

Often times we will not communicate with our loved ones. We will expect them to read our minds, and we will have an expectation of how they should respond or be there for us and when they don't respond the way we would like or are not there for us, we breakdown.

Explore your language, your thought process and areas in your body that feel contracted or painful. Practice being mindful of what you are communicating and how you are communicating it. Let this be a week of speaking your truth in a way that is loving and accepting of yourself and others. Pay attention to the words you are using and if it is uplifting or downgrading. As we begin to consciously choose to be guided by the highest vision for our lives, we will naturally begin to move away from anything that is not in alignment with it.

Notes and Reflections

26. If there is something missing, I do the best I can to articulate and express who and what I am, and what it is that I need or desire

Life gives us a continual opportunity to refine and redesign. We never arrive to a particular place and say, "I'm all done here. There's no more growth or learning." It's a journey of uncovering, questioning, and exploring, and once we recognize this, we find that there is always an opportunity to look in the mirror and ask if something is missing.

If there is something missing in any area of life—whether it is the relationship with myself or others, with my health, career or contribution—it is my responsibility to find the discipline, commitment, motivation, passion, and/or solution. How you articulate and express yourself is controlled by no one. Do we sometimes give our power to others or shrink in the presence of others—absolutely we do and that does not mean that others are responsible for our results. That is actually part of the standing in your power and owning your life and your purpose. You and you alone are responsible for your life, your relationships, and your results, and when you make a commitment to yourself to *be yourself* and to express authentically, there will be a strength and power that rise up to meet that higher consciousness.

What is your desire? What wants to express? All too often, when we write our goals and vision, in many cases it is the vision of others or what we think they want or expect of us. We want to make them proud; we never want to disappoint or let anyone down.

What still wants to be expressed? What in you wants to come alive, wants to be a part of something bigger? What do you desire to become?

Maybe it's all outlined in your vision and maybe it's a brand-new desire to express even more fully. Let that desire, that impulse, that passion, that feeling rise up within you. *Have it!* Let your ideas and imagination give birth to whatever it is inside of you that is calling to express. The very word "De-Sire" is Latin meaning "of the Father." In other words, it is gifted to you from the Father—of Spirit, God, or Source. Call it what you will; there is no denying it, and it is an authentic, meaningful, powerful gift that you are worthy of having. If it wasn't intended to be you, you wouldn't have the desire.

Make no mistake; our true, authentic desires that are of the Father, hurt no one. They do not exploit or disempower others. They do not cheat, lie, steal, or give false information. They are born of the heart and are only for good. Do not attempt to use, take advantage, hurt, destroy, or cause harm to anyone or anything. You will reap what you sow. You have free will and you will do whatever you wish; however, you are not free from the consequences of your choices.

We, each one of us—are the hands and feet of God—the ones who have the honor and privilege to live full out—to Be, Do and Have everything we desire. When we decide to lead from the heart, life will give us opportunities beyond our belief. How will you let your desire lead you and what opportunities might lie ahead if you asked for support in areas where you feel that something is missing or depleted?

Let this be a time of focus. Ask yourself: How can I and how will I express even more fully? I will pay attention to the desires and impulses that rise up within me, and I will let them have their way. I will make that call, reach out, investigate, search, find, discover, and accept all of the good feelings, ideas, and support that shows up.

Notes and Reflections

Let every deisre have its way with you-
it is yours purposfully.
Given to you of the father.
There is no one else,
no one to do it better,
and no one more worthy.
Your desire is your heart's song.
It is the message, the book, the dance,
and the dream.
It is your calling and your soul's journey.
It is your full expression—
Completely and authentically yours.
Let it have its way with you.
Anchor into this truth
and allow nothing and no one
to keep you from it.
It is yours to do.

Sylvia Castillo

27. There is no story writing

How often do we write a story about something and make up the worst possible conclusion? Someone is late or they don't call back right away, someone doesn't respond in the way that we think they should, or we don't get the feedback were looking for—and then we make up a story about what that means and how we feel about it. We project our own insecurities and then are afraid to talk about how we feel. The crazy thing is: in the moment we get frustrated and upset; we actually have a physical response in our body, that puts our system on high alert. Toxins are released in the body and biochemically there is a negative cocktail brewing within. Automatically, we feel into this story, and once the mind connects with the negative cocktail, it takes over and we are done. We will find evidence and proof to support our thinking. We will pull in memories, past hurts, and the opinion of others that have nothing to do with it. And this fuels the story. We will not only create the story, we will give life to it and forecast the next six months, including all the ways will get revenge, and we will stay in a pattern of depression, lack, limitation, scarcity, and aloneness—*And it's all made up!*

    Sometimes we say to another person, "you made me…" as if we were a puppet and that someone else has control over making us do anything. We may give our power away, or we may be so caught up in the drama of things that we think someone made us pissed off, or pushed our buttons so much that it caused us to react in a certain way. We actually say to them, "You made me this way." Immediately we are thrown into resistance, resentment, and revenge—and the game is back on.

The invitation is to really begin to see how this plays out in our lives as self-sabotage, damaged relationships, and ongoing drama. What if instead of writing a story that made everyone wrong, we decided to pay more attention to how we are feeling and responding. Let us begin to connect with what is going on within our own mind and body. We really do choose moment by moment how we are going to show up, what we will be committed to and how we will respond in any given situation.

When we become the best version of ourselves that we can be, we don't need to cut people out of our lives or make them responsible for our results. Our opportunity is to focus on our own self-care, the quality of our relationships, our career, and contribution. We get to stand as an example for others—and they will decide to rise up to their own potential or to find another playground of drama. Here's the deal about growth—not everyone wants to participate. It is not easy to look in the mirror and take 100% responsibility for your life. It is a lifetime commitment, and we have to make a daily commitment to stay on track. Not everyone is ready for that kind of responsibility. It is not your job to attempt to fix others or to even see them as less than or whatever story we could make up about that too. Our job is to stay committed to our own path and to find the people and support that we need for our own growth and expansion.

Proclaim: I will pay attention to the stories I am making up. I will be the witness and just notice where my thinking and BEing is. In moments that I find myself getting disturbed, I will take a few minutes to take a few deep breaths, and I will remember to anchor in my vision. The opportunity is to be the witness and to keep noticing where I am placing my attention. Am I in my head making up worst case sinearo or am I staying on track?

Notes and Reflections

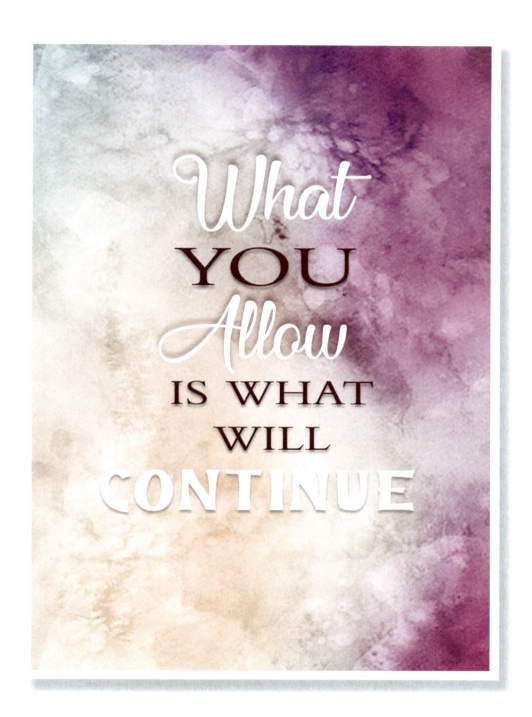

28. I will not create my own doubt, animosity, confusion, illusion, bitterness, suspicion, or conflict based on speculation

As we begin the deliberate practice of being a creator in our own lives, we continue to explore and implement new practices that will help in moving and shifting our perspective and grounding in such a way that we are not moved from our own sense of purpose. The truth is that each one of us is a unique, powerful, and amazing blessing, and as we stay committed to a path of growth, we will be more intentional about the way we show up in the world. When we get really committed to our personal vision (the one created from our hearts desire), we won't have room or time to write stories or stay in drama that keep us off track.

Last week the goal was to notice our thinking and BEingness and to be mindful of what stories we were making up. How often did doubt, animosity, confusion, illusion, bitterness, suspicion, or conflict come up? How often were there reasons and excuses that kept the vision on pause while your attention was placed on everything besides what you said you wanted?

There are so many distractions, and if it's not our own story writing, it's the stories of other people. Often times we make their drama our own, we get so wrapped up in their stuff that our time is consumed with everyone and everything besides our own vision. Add to the mix the importance we place on posting, tweeting, snapping, and chatting, there goes all of the extra time we had to work on our goals, dreams, and vision.

It will be our discipline and commitment that determine whether or not we get what we say we want. It comes down to the choices we are making about everything and in every area of our lives. It's a day by day and sometimes a moment by moment decision. The question will always come back to me to: What am I committed to and what are the choices that am I making?

The journey is ongoing, and the opportunities are endless—and the moment that that we get clear about our life, our vision, and our value—once we accept it and own it as our opportunity and our responsibility, we will get excited about every choice that we are making.

Affirm to yourself: I will get focused, and my doubt will be channeled into direction, my animosity will be replaced with adaptability, confusion will be transformed into conscious choice making. The thin veil of my illusions will finally fall away, and my bitterness will become happiness. Suspicion will be saturated with all things good, and in harmony with my highest vision and conflict will fuel my creativity to find solutions. The only thing that I will speculate and ponder on is that **if it is to be it is up to me**!

Everything from this point forward will be intentional. From the way I see the world to the things I choose to be involved in, I will lean into my fears, and I will come to know them in a deep and intimate way. I recognize that there truly is nothing and no one that keeps me from my good, and I will continue to release anything that keep me from my highest good.

I will pay attention to the stories that I am writing, and my ongoing self-talk. I will be intentional about the stories I am writing and if I'm going to write them anyway, I am going to make it good!

Notes and Reflections

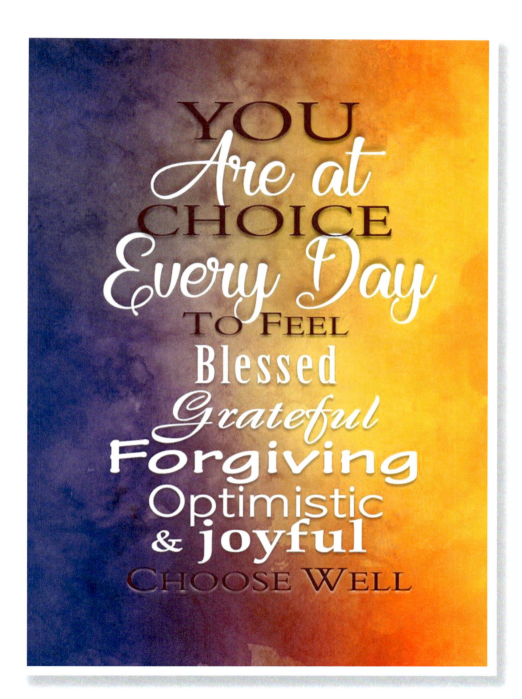

29. I am clear and conscious

The definition of clear is free from darkness, obscurity, or cloudiness, and that is exactly where we are headed—to be authentic so that our thoughts, feelings, and actions are in alignment. We will discover that being transparent means that I can tell my story—good or bad, right or wrong without fear or anxiety of being rejected. When I am conscious, it means that I have decided to be fully awake, aware, and alive—and to fully participate in life. It's deciding that I am worthy and capable, and that I choose to be trusting, trustworthy and full in.

We know that the words "I AM" are critical—because whatever, we say after "I am," will be. So, beginning now, this is the foundation and the affirmations I set for myself.

I am safe

I belong

I am smart

I am loved

I am enough

I am important

I have something to contribute

I am not alone

I am safe, and even if there are things that happen that are outside of my control, I will not be a casualty to them.

I belong. I know that I belong because I am here. My contribution matters, and I am valuable.

I am smart. I have an intelligence and internal guidance system that lives within me, and I am a powerful creator in my life.

I am enough. I affirm my strength, intelligence, and personal power. I understand that life is for and never against me, and I have all of the support I need. Life is good.

I am important. In this amazing tapestry of life, my role and my vision matters.

I have something to contribute; it's more than just an idea. It's a desire that lives within my heart. It's the part of me that continues grow. I am committed to greatness.

I am not alone. I am loved and surrounded by those who see me bigger than I see myself. They challenge, encourage and inspire me.

I step into the great I AM with enthusiasm. I recognize that I AM a powerful co-creator in this life, and I choose to see what's good and what's working. I am in the process of transformation, and I give thanks for the blessings of new experiences, knowing fear, and saying yes.

When my dear friend Jessica created a vision for her life, including the marriage of her dreams, she was faced with the realization that her current reality was not in alignment with her highest vision. She was in a marriage that didn't have the qualities that she believed a healthy, vibrant, collaborative, passionate marriage could have.

As she struggled with this realization, she searched tirelessly in every way she could to find answers and solutions to make it work. She and her husband never had children, and they thought that having a child might give their lives the change and upliftment she craved.

They decided to adopt; however, once they went through all the processes and paperwork to get approved, Jessica couldn't go through with it. She knew that bringing a child into an unfulfilled marriage was not the answer.

Her soul was calling out for expansion, her intuition was speaking to her as loudly as it could—reminding her that there was more to life than what she was experiencing, and she knew that leaving her relationship was the only option.

It was not an easy decision, and it wasn't a decision that she made overnight. It was a conscious uncoupling; in other words, it was two people who loved each other enough to let go of a relationship that was not growing together or expanding in ways that bring fulfillment.

The "Transformation" writing below was written for her. Because in every way she had to embrace and know all of her fears. She came to know that she was safe, that she belonged, and that she was smart. She knew she was enough, that she was not alone, and that she was important and had something to contribute. Once she made a decision to accept the Truth about herself, Transformation was inevitable.

She awoken with clarity,
unlike anything she had ever known.
When she looked in the mirror,
she began to weep because she knew the
life she had been living
was not the life that was calling her.

In a moment, every decision
she was about to make would alter
her life in every way.
Nothing would remain the same.
In her moments of weakness, she questioned,
and in her moments of clarity, she knew.

She was in the midst of transformation,
and her vision was pulling her;
her heart was opening, her soul was calling,
and her path was unfolding.

Every story, every excuse
and every doubt, began to dissolve…
and in its place, was certainty.
As she anchored into this truth
the colors of her Love began to appear—
bright with passion, beautifully complex
and vivid with purpose and direction.

Before us, in all of her beauty,
she is renewed, restored and reawakened.
Finally accepting the miracle and the magic
she brings to this life.
And she soars—
ever awakening, always evolving
and forever expanding.
She is light, she is love,
and she is home.
The gifts of courage
and trust and transformation
are the blessings she brings with her
wherever she goes.
And she is free~

Sylvia Castillo

30. I use my time, my energy, and my voice for resolution and solution

My time is precious, and I will use it wisely. I will do what is hard first, and I will also remember to acknowledge myself and continue to celebrate my wins along the way. I've decided to believe that things are always happening for me and not to me. From this perspective, I see clearly. When I get committed, I recognize that there is no time to waste and that I must be disciplined in the things that I give my time and attention to.

As I continue to grow in all areas of my life, I see that staying committed to my goals and dreams requires me to have an intention and to focus my attention on the things that matter. If I give my time to something that is not moving me forward on my vision, I must re-evaluate. I understand that personal growth and development is a constant opportunity to refine and re-evaluate *and* to stay true to myself.

Being committed to resolution means that I don't allow myself to stay in fear, conflict or confusion. Although things will come up and I may be challenged, I don't have a pity party for myself, and I don't stay in resistance, resentement or revenge (for very long).

I see myself as a creator, one who is powerful. I have options and as I continue on this path of the agreements I have with myself, I can hear my self-talk changing. It is a voice of good and of possibility. I see that there is support and solutions all around me. I am an advocate for myself, and I don't have expectations of others to make sure I'm ok. I will ask for guidance and support when I need it. I will accept feedback and constructive criticism because it helps me grow and gives valuable contrast.

I remember to surrender in moments of chaos because the only thing I can control is my response. I choose to be vulnerable because sometimes the most amazing connections with others come from our ability to really see another person. I get that when I give, communicate, participate, and stay humble—when I do my own work, my relationships begin to support every aspect of my life.

Using my voice for resolution and solution gives me an opportunity to gain clarity and direction like never before. I make a conscious commitment to be engaged. I decide to operate to from true choice; in other words choosing to be authentic and true to myself—saying "yes" only when I mean "yes" and knowing that saying "no" supports me best when I am overcommitted and not when I am avoiding something or someone.

Life gives me a series of opportunities to show up—to use my voice, my heart, my intellect, my energy, my hands, and feet, gifts and talents—to be a participant, to show up, and to make a difference. I keep saying "yes" to that.

I will pay close attention to where I am saying "yes" and to what and who gets my time and attention. I am mindful about where I am placing my focus and what I am committed to. Is it serving me? Is it inspiring me? Is it growing me? Is it getting me closer to my vision?

Notes and Reflections

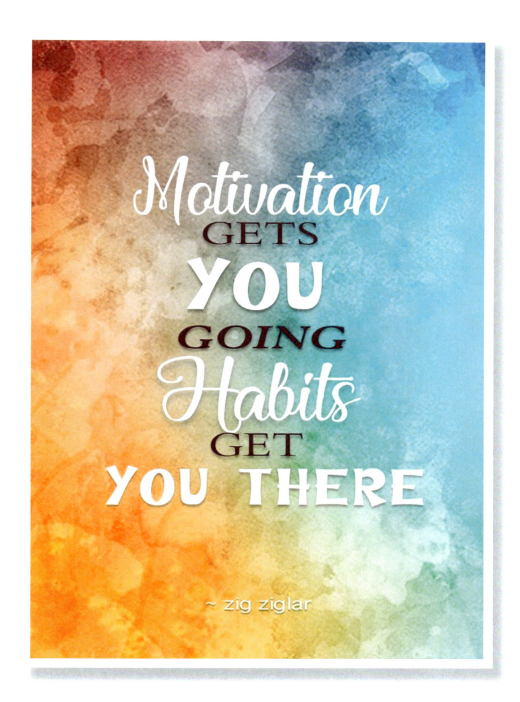

31. I am committed to greatness

Your vision is filled with everything that is important to you. It is a blueprint and a road map to your own personal greatness. The choices you make day by day and moment by moment will determine whether or not you stay on the path that will lead you to your destination. Make no mistake, you came here to be great and you do have the ultimate say as to how you will be great and when you will allow it to happen. For some, it will in their last breath, as they return home to the love that brought them here.

Life is the ultimate opportunity. We are given dominion over our thoughts, we have free choice and free will, we live in an infinite universe with unlimited possibility—and we are sourced with a power and presence that breathes us, guides and directs us, and all we have to do is listen and say "yes."

It is everything else that gets in the way. Our stories and limiting beliefs, our commitment to lack and limitation, and our fear of getting uncomfortable.

Remember the old saying that graveyards are the richest lands of them all because the are filled with books, ideas, inventions, dreams, and visions that never came to be. Wouldn't *now* be a good time to honestly get so committed to your greatness and vision that literally nothing and no one would keep you from it?!

Often times things will happen that are outside of our control. We will experience natural disasters, loss, separation, death, and divorce among the many other things that can and will occur. Although they are a part of what we all experience, they don't have to be the end of our dreams or the new victim story that we get so used to telling. These occurrences have a great significance on our lives, and we will make either make a choice to let them negatively define us, or we will find the gift and use it to make a difference.

When we really get how much we matter and how great we really are, we will begin to honor our path and our vision in such a way that it becomes the benchmark and the line in the sand for everything that is yet to be. We could hardly know the great plans in store for us as we lay down our weapons of destruction, words of limitation, and our fears of being amazing.

Say to yourself: I affirm my ultimate good, and I am committed to greatness. I trust my inner guidance and I let that power and that strength guide and direct me.

I stay honest with myself, and I pay attention to when I feel alive with enthusiasm and when I am excited about my vision. I will spend more time with those people and those places that support my goals and vision. I commit and recommit daily to taking action, to being on purpose, and to doing the little things that all add up.

One decision at a time and one step at a time, I am committed to Greatness!

Notes and Reflections

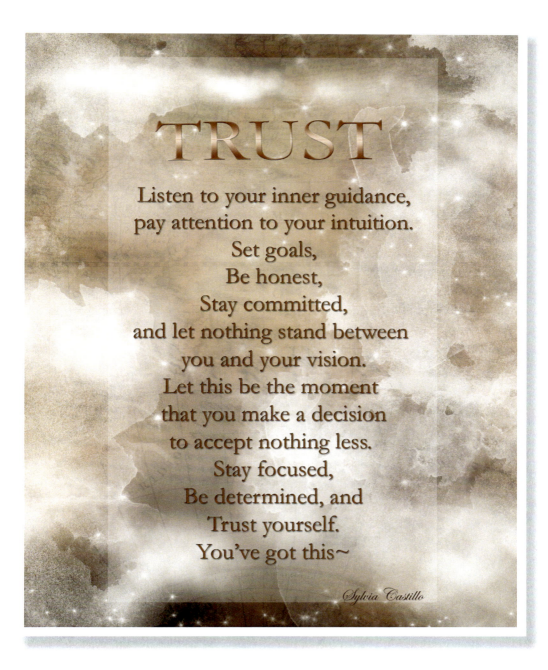

32. I will do the best I can

Doing the best I can is such a personal statement—one that cannot be compared with anyone or anything else. My own personal best is something only I have control of.

Isn't it interesting how some days you can wake up on fire with purpose, so committed to taking positive action, absolutely clear about what needs to be accomplished and unquestionably determined to make things happen. Aren't they amazing?! We feel so powerful, awake, aware, and alive. Those are the days and moments that we are so grounded in knowing who we are and where we're going that we don't question.

We just BE. We are in the moment, we feel inspired, and life feels good.

And then there are the other days—the days that we forget. The experience is the exact opposite. Getting out of bed is a struggle, getting motivated is impossible, and getting on track with life feels hopeless. It's discouraging and sometimes it seems like we're the only ones who ever feel this way. We go for the phone immediately and check all social media accounts to compare notes, and of course, everything looks perfect in social media land.

I promise you it is not what it appears to be. We all, each one of us—has those days, moments and sometimes years, of feeling like we are wandering in the desert. Some might say that those times are brought on as punishment, and sometimes it feels like punishment; however, it's a natural consequence of what happens when our intention and attention is the wrong place *and* it is in those moments of contrast, of what is and what is wanted, that give us the opportunity to declare, decide, and devote ourselves to something different.

When we start to pay close attention to the things that we are focusing on, we will notice that we feel the way we feel because of the thoughts we are thinking and what we are focusing on. Tony Robbins, a renowned author, philanthropist, and life coach has an exercise on focus. He says, look around the room you are in and find everything that is brown. Look hard, look closely and look fast— you only have another minute to take it all in. Now close your eyes and tell me everything you saw that was blue and green. It's almost impossible right? If you were focusing on everything that was brown and everything that looked like shit, you didn't see what was blue and green, you missed out on so much. So the same it goes with life, notice what is being missed because of where the focus is.

When I commit to *be* the best I can, I am intentional. I pay attention to what I am focused on. I keep myself accountable to positive action and quitting is not an option. I recognize that loving myself, staying grounded, expressing gratitude, and staying in integrity are all requirements.

It's hard to know exactly where we would end up if we chose to add a even only a 1% shift to what we are committed to. If I were flying a from JFK to LAX and I were 1% off course, I would be nearly fifty miles from my destination. Consider this: Imagine what would be possible if doing the best I can meant giving just a little bit more. What could I or would I possibly create?!

I am committed to doing the best I can. I will stay on track with my goals, my vision, and my life everywhere possible. I'll give a little more than before.

Notes and Reflections

Imagine

What a beautiful transformation into the light-
The awakening....
the story of Truth
in all of Its perfection.
You have come here to be the Alchemist-
to be the Scientist,
and to use this Life as your laboratory.
You have come here to learn Acceptance
in such an amazing way,
and to recognize that you have an inner strength
and an inner wisdom that
Guides and Protects you Always!
You are a Light
with The Power of A Thousand Suns.
Stake your claim to this Truth
and allow it to be embodied
deep within you.
It is all that you need...

Sylvia Castillo

33. and I start with me

I will do the best I can, and I start with me. It all starts with me, and in the moment that I decide that it is up to me, that there is nothing and no one standing between me and my highest vision. Everything changes.

I recognize that no one has power over me, and if there is any place within me that feels negatively triggered by another, it's time for me to look within. If I desire a loving, generous, prosperous, and healthy life, I cannot simultaneously wish harm on others and/or be wrapped up in drama. I will stand firmly planted, anchored to my truth and the vision for my life. I am in charge of me, and I choose where I will place my life's energy and focus.

When I start with me, I lead without judgment. I don't fear meeting others even if they don't share the same background, color, religion, opinion, beliefs, or sexual orientation. I choose to be accepting of all people because that is the ultimate opportunity because we really are brothers and sisters in one human family. I will be outwardly focused, the first one to extend a genuine smile, the first one to call, the first to say hello or lend a helping hand or needed friend. I'll be the first to apologize and the first to assume the best. The first to make amends and the first to forgive. I will be brave and vulnerable. I will give lots of grace and tolerance because there will come a time when I may need it too.

When we activate our bravery, claim our vision, and allow ourselves to be guided by our hearts wisdom, we will be transformed, and it will be a blessing to all of those around us.

As we begin to care about ourselves and others in such a way that everything matters, we become solution oriented and everything becomes an opportunity. Even as challenges come up. They do not consume us. In fact, we being to prepare for the best outcome, looking again at all of the areas of our life. We become even more intentional about how we will steward and manage our responsibilities.

We get diligent about discovering what habits we have that are moving us toward our goals, and we become even more disciplined in the way we manage our time so that there are no excuses for not moving toward the vision.

Life begins to offer up the opportunity for me to engage my humor, to ignite my passion, to tap into my resources, to turn on my excitement, and to tune into the truth. And the truth is that its been there all along. It was me who's been out of alignment, focused on the opposite of what I desire, and blocking the flow of my own good.

It's just like the radio station. If I am tuned into FM 98.6 and I don't like what's playing, the only way that I can hear something different is to tune into another station. It's actually more than a station, it is a frequency, and I am tuning into a new frequency. One of possibility, prosperity, abundance, liberty and joy.

Affirm: Today, I am open to receive. I recognize that life is always conspiring for my greater good, and I lovingly invite that goodness to move to and through me.

I will do the best I can, and I start with me.

Notes and Reflections

DISCOVER

As you begin to grow and discover,
you will find that
nothing looks the same-
and as you close your eyes
and open your heart,
you will begin to sense and feel
that everything around you is changing.
Say yes,
and in the surrender
allow every fear, every doubt,
and every uncertainty to
be embraced by the
Divine love and
Divine guidance that
lives and moves and
breathes as you.
Life is calling for you
to grow, to become, and
to discover the Beautiful,
Compassionate,
Capable
You.

Sylvia Castillo

34. I will love, honor, and nurture, myself

What an amazing invitation—to be able to love, honor, and nurture myself. What are all the ways that I will express this to myself? They say that we cannot love another until we come to love and accept ourselves. This is such a profound statement—the very thing that I wish to have, to be loved and accepted. I must give to myself first and then give it away. It is here in this place of vulnerability and authenticity where I really begin to "feel" the transformation.

This is the place where I could see and love you regardless of what you've done, or where you've been or what mistakes you've made. I see into the eyes of your soul, I see the pain of regret and the hope of acceptance, and I love you because I see myself in you. So, I choose to love and forgive myself so that I can love and forgive you.

Many times, it is in our deepest pain and regret that we begin to loosen the chains of judgment and bondage. We may have been self-righteous, impatient, arrogant, or have created unrealistic expectations. In any case, once we make a decision to "Be the One," there are no more excuses. I love and accept myself right where I am, and I love and accept you right where you are. This is not to say that I don't want more, better, or different for you. I just recognize that is a personal journey that you will have with yourself.

There is a term called "self-referral" which means when looking for acceptance and approval, I refer to myself; in other words, I look within for that guidance. This is the opposite of "object-referral" which is to look outside of myself, or in another, for approval. When I operate from "self-referral," I don't need someone else to make sure that I'm ok. I look to myself. I recognize and know that I am enough and that I have everything I need within me.

I honor myself by holding the high watch. I keep my word, I have a standard of integrity, and I am true to myself. I live with principles and values. I move daily towards my goals and dreams, and I push myself to be the best version of myself that I can be.

I remember that that I am love and that I am made in the image of love. I remember that love is patient, love is kind. It does not envy, it does not boast, it is not proud. It is not rude, it is not self-seeking, it is not easily angered, it keeps no record of wrongs. Love rejoices in the truth. It always protects, always trusts, always hopes, always perseveres. Love never fails.

I practice being a loving person and seeing others as loving people as well.

I consider how love could be an elixir for everything I encounter. I make it a priority to nurture myself with spending time outdoors in nature and by making time to treat myself to getting pampered in the ways that feel special to me. I connect with purpose, desiring always to be honest, authentic, and loving. I make a personal devotion to and daily practice to love, honor, and nurture myself.

I get realigned with my Spiritual practices, and I stay committed to taking care of me.

Regarding Spiritual practices: if you do not have a spiritual home, church, place, or group of people who have similar beliefs about God, Love, and Contribution (whatever that means for you), the opportunity is to find one. Making time to share and explore this part of ourselves is essential. When we have a Spiritual groundedness, and when we anchor to deeper truth about ourselves, we are less likely to look outward for permission to grow or approval to be ourselves.

Notes and Reflections

35. I will take care of my needs

As I continue to commit to a life of growth and expansion I will pay attention to my needs.

If you have ever been aboard an airplane, you have seen a presentation on safety. You are specifically told that if for any reason an oxygen mask drops from the overhead compartment, you are to put on your oxygen mask first and then take care of the needs of others. It's pretty clear that if we do put the mask on first, we would not only endanger our own life, it would be impossible to take care of anyone else.

It is important to take care of our needs, and yet, there is also an opportunity here to recognize how we show up. Ask: Am I only committed to taking of myself?

Do I completely disregard myself to take care of others? Do I take care of myself so that I can also be available for someone else? Or do I completely disregard my needs altogether? Where in my life do I have the opportunity to take care of me first? This is not to say that the needs of others won't be met; rather, it is a commitment to stay aware of how I am feeling and meeting my own needs.

What are my beliefs about how I take care of myself and others? Is it "normal" to feel stressed and have anxiety? Do I feel more needed when I am overcommitted? Does putting myself first make me feel like I'm not there for others? Or that I need to spend time taking care of others first because that is my job?

Exploring these questions and being aware of the challenges or obstacles we have in regard to our taking care of our own needs will give us an opportunity let go of limiting beliefs, ideas, thoughts, and behaviors.

There are many ways to nourish ourselves. How we wake up and commit to the day is an essential part of meeting our needs. When our day starts with deliberate intention for quiet time, prayer, and/or meditation, we connect to our source in such a way that we feel grounded and anchored. When we feel that sense of connectedness, we are less likely to be moved from feeling centered when we experience challenges, problems, and obstacles. In fact, as we continue to focus on our vision and create our day from a place of being purposeful, we experience a sense of fulfillment, excitement, and clarity that we may have never felt before.

Adding exercise to our routine is another essential self-care opportunity. There is a mind, body, soul connection, and as we make time for walking, yoga, weights, and all of the other ways we nourish the body, we will have increased energy and vitality. We know that when we feel good in our bodies, it positively affects our mood, intimacy and overall *beingness*.

Being aware and open to all of the ways that we can take care of ourselves will definitely add to our overall experience of life. When I take time to listen to my loved ones, when my household, my finances' and my work is in order, when I take a social media break and plan my life, I increase the peace within me. I worry less, play more, and I build a life on the infinite possibilities that are available to me. My perspective shifts into creator of my life and author of my story. Its empowering and powerful.

Consider: How are all the ways I will take care of myself? What am I doing really good at and where is there room for improvement? Life gives us an opportunity every single day to refine, remember, and commit to positive action. What will be the focus of my week, and where will I being to make shifts that continue to align with the highest vision for my life?

Notes and Reflections

SENDING YOU LOTS OF LOVE AS YOU EMBRACE YOUR TRUTH

There will come a day when nothing will remain the same,
and it is in this moment
that you will recognize that your Life is waiting for you…
You will begin the journey of self discovery;
you will learn that thoughts become things, that beliefs will hold you or mold you,
and you will come to understand the power of your word.

There will be gratitude for every person, every circumstance,
every trial and tribulation, every dream and desire-
and you will come to know that you are a creator-
and in this awaking you will begin to uncover the amazing gifts from heaven.

I pray that in this moment
you let your burning desire set the world on fire,
that you come to love yourself,
forgive yourself and BE yourself.
May you look beyond what the eyes can see
and come to know that this is a magical universe,
and as you become deliberate, as you set an intention for your life,
you will gain clarity and your vision will be placed before you as an undeniable path.

Your wisdom is within you— your heritage, your lineage, your parents,
your people- it is all purposeful and more than that it's beautiful and powerful.
It's learning and growing, it's challenging and exhilarating, it's hurtful and
harmonious, it's painful and wonderful, it's complex and graceful,
and it is the natural ebb and flow.

The elixir of life is upon you, and it is in the revealing of this truth that you will
be set free. You have abundance, health and harmony.
You are perfect, whole, and complete in every way.
You have come here on a journey of self-discovery,
and in the moment that you let your imagination run free, your inspiration to move
you, and your intuition guide you, life will never look the same.

And it is here, in this sweet surrender where Love will have its way.
When you will look upon all things with gratitude and thanksgiving,
where you will come to know the truth that has been true always.
It is here, heaven upon earth in this infinite possibility called you.
May you awaken to this truth, may you bless this life and the world you live in,
and may you always remember.

And So It Is.

~Sylvia Castillo

36. protect my space (I will)

Personal development is not a top priority for everyone. People get set in their ways; they are buried in their pain, numbed out, in avoidance or choose to be complacent and comfortable. For their own reasons, they choose to make choices for their life that keep them distanced, angry, and/or separated. There are so many reasons, excuses, and all kinds of stories to support limiting beliefs. Much of it is about self-preservation and protection. It's a defense mechanism to stay safe and to avoid our perceived pain.

When we protect our space, we can do so without condemning anyone. We don't need to make others wrong. There is no need to be self-righteous or to throw stones.

Rather, we simply choose love, acceptance, and possibility over everything else.

Our time is spent making a conscious choice to be and stay in alignment with ourselves. We choose to extend unconditional love and acceptance in all that we do.

Protecting our space does not mean building a wall so high and far around us that no one and nothing could find their way in. It's more about our inner landscape. To protect our inner self would be to anchor, meditate, and pray so often that even when things are difficult, we remember that people or circumstances beyond our control do not define us, positively or negatively.

It's important to notice and differentiate protecting our space and avoiding a growth opportunity with another person. There is a fine line between writing someone off and creating a loving boundary.

More often than not, we will write others off and chalk it up to taking care of ourselves. The opportunity is to seek to understand

and to be the witness—even if that is your angry ex, the sibling that no longer talks to you, parent(s) who were checked out, your defiant children, or your old best friend. Anger and hate that is projected on another is our own unresolved pain. Blaming and shaming others only postpones the opportunity to grow and what remains unforgiven is poison to our own soul.

Sometimes what we fail to notice is that our programs, ego/protective personality is always in reactive mode. It doesn't think or reason; it is the judge and executor. It's important to remember, we are arguing with someone else's programs—not the truth of who they are. When we operate from a space of non-resistance, we recognize that someone we once loved and cared for went straight to defensive mode and is operating from fight or flight. When we are truly grounded, we are able to separate the behavior or attitude from the person.

A loving boundary might look like not allowing someone to share your space or your home if they are violating it. It's not ok to make excuses for a behavior that hurts other people, and at the same time writing that person off removes the opportunity to extend love and forgiveness. If we have negative energy on a person and we think that just writing them off will fix everything, don't be fooled; it's not the same thing. Unforgiveness is the cause of much anxiety and depression. More often than not forgiveness is the solution or elixir that is needed. It is also important to recognize that someone does not need to be present in their physical form in order for us to extend love and forgiveness.

There are people that we will be connected with for a lifetime through our families and marriages. We won't always see eye to eye. In fact, we may disagree completely, and we can still love and respect another person, even when we don't agree with them.

Protecting our space means taking a stand for growth and expansion. It is aligning with a bigger vision and a knowingness that we are either growing or dying. There is no in-between. We can choose without judgement to align ourselves with others who also want grow. "Birds of a feather flock together," and we can be committed to protecting and cultivation our space of peace, growth, contribution, and development.

Let us also be mindful of protecting ourselves from our own "monkey mind." If there were one thing that we would want to master in this lifetime, it would be conscious choice making and mental mastery. As we deliberately direct our thoughts, we become less and less reactive. When our minds become a servant of our hearts, when our decisions are heart-driven, we are on the right path.

Today, I will continue look for opportunities to build and strengthen relationships. I will take another inventory of my space both mentally and physically, make amends, and pay close attention to my vibe and my tribe. And I will extend unconditional love.

37. expand my consciousness (I will)

Our consciousness is the sum total of everything we have ever believed, everything we have felt a conviction about, and everything we have learned. Because consciousness is causation—meaning it is causal and will bring to us those experiences that are in alignment with our thinking and beingness—it is important to recognize where our tendency is. Are you hanging out in lack, limitation, and not—enoughness, or are you in abundance, excitement, and possibility?

Wherever we are operating from, whatever that tendency is, that determines how much of the unlimited supply of good will flow to and through us, and we will attract to ourselves experiences and circumstances that are equal to or in alignment with it. Author and Mindfulness Expert, Dennis Merritt Jones says it like this: "Your consciousness goes before you to announce that you are coming".

We are not separate from our creator; we are children of the most high, made from and in the image and likeness of It. Call It what you will—there is a power within us—whether we recognize it or not and whether we use it or not. It is the same intelligence that turns an acorn into an oak tree, it is the rising of the sun, the turning of every tide. It is every blade of grass and every grain of sand. IT is the very breath that breathes and sustains us in every single moment. It is trillions of cells and multiple organs that work in perfect harmony to animate and individualize each one of us. Understand that consciousness speaks to this creative power and our bodies and our personal awareness are expressions of this Infinite Oneness. When we get that each one of us is individually and uniquely created from this Source, that we are the hands and feet of ITs good, then our perspective of everything changes. Everything becomes an opportunity.

The question then becomes: How will I cultivate this place of love, peace, and unlimited possibility within me? To expand my consciousness would be to increase my understanding and acceptance of my worthiness, my wholeness, and the flow of my life in size, volume, and scope—to literally stretch out and unfold like a bird that expands its wings to soar. It means that I will claim my good in fuller form and in greater detail and to recognize that I am ever evolving.

Our experiences and our realities reflect our consciousness, and this is wonderful news because we get to affirm, choose, and create our reality. We're it! We are the ones we've been waiting for! As we learn more about Universal Laws such as cause and effect, mental equivalence, the law of circulation, and the undeniable power of Love, we choose then how we will be a player in this game of life.

Contemplate this: Our Spiritual practices are essential in expanding our consciousness; when I live, move, and have my being in an abundant Source that knows nothing of lack and limitation, what then might I create? Today, this knowingness energizes me. I am inspired and continue to expand my consciousness.

Notes and Reflections

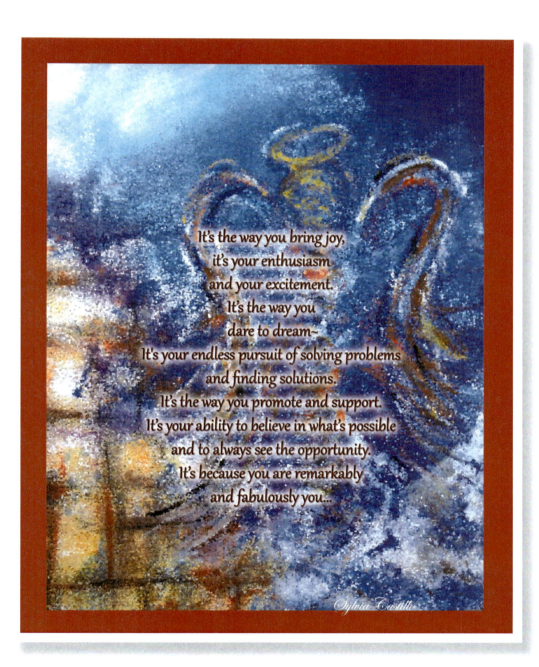

38. exercise my body and shape my life (I will)

It's important to know that who I am is not my body. My body is the shell of me, it is what houses the Truth of me, the Soul and Spirit of me, and yet because I have a body and because it is the vehicle that I get to use for this human experience, my relationship to it is extremely important. How I treat it, what I put into it, and how I move it matters.

Moving our bodies whether it be dance, exercise, rock climbing, yoga, or the many other ways we move and strengthen our bodies is a vital part of the way we feel.

When we make a decision and a commitment to take care of it, it will take care of us.

The amazing thing about exercise are the benefits; it can make you feel happier and actually decreases feelings of anxiety and depression. It helps with weight loss, and for many of us losing that extra 10-30 pounds not only changes our pant or dress size, it also positively affects our confidence and morale. There is no doubt that it increases our energy and vitality, and when we feel strong and powerful, we show up in our lives from a completely different place compared to when we feel lethargic and out of shape. Exercise also reduces the risk of chronic disease and can improve skin and brain health. It helps with our quality of relaxation and sleep as well as reducing pain. Exercise and combined weight loss can also positively affect our intimacy and the way we show up with our spouse or significant other. If you've ever wanted to keep the lights off or stay under the covers because you didn't want your partner to see you, then you understand the significance of this statement.

Sometimes the excuse is not having enough time, knowledge, or courage to do something new and/or different. And often times we have to say "no" to something else so that we can say "yes" to this. When the alarm goes off, the challenge is to get right up, no snoozing.

Waking up with intention plays a key role in our personal evolution.

It also comes back to discipline. Like everything else, we must be willing to look at our level of commitment and the discipline it will take to have what we say we want.

How you decide to shape your life will impact everything. When our bodies are aligned with our highest vision, we have amazing amounts of energy and vitality. We are literally changing on the outside to match what's on the inside. The discoveries and sense of purpose are exciting and give new life and enthusiasm to all that you do.

Imagine what you will do in that new body of yours?! The energy and vitality you feel are incredible! You have never felt more alive than you do right now. Late night dancing and early—morning lovemaking with the lights on is just the tip of the iceberg. You never imagined that feeling this good would impact your work and your social life too. People keep saying how great you look, and you feel like a million bucks. This is how it feels to be on fire with passion, you feel like there is nothing you can't to and it is incredible! *So* good!

Affirm: I am committed to feeling this way about myself, my body, and my life.

Today, I practice taking care of my body and shaping a life that I am excited to live in.

Notes and Reflections

39. I will give time to the things that inspire and bring joy to me

Sometimes we have dreams and ideas about what we want to be doing with our lives, and as we contemplate these things they inspire us. There is an overwhelming sense of joy, and we feel great about what we have an intention to create.

It's good to recognize and know that these desires of the heart are ours purposefully. Even if there are others in the world doing what you have an idea to do, it doesn't matter. No one has the creative output, voice, heart, intention, skill, attitude, knowledge, and drive exactly like you. Sometimes people ask, "How do I know?" or "How can I trust that its mine to do?".

Here's the answer for that—If it's on your heart and it doesn't go away, it's yours to do.

Where desire meets intention,
vision becomes reality.

When your intention is clear, when you *know*, when you have a *certainty* about what it is that is yours to do, and it is born of a desire of the heart, it *will* become your reality.

It is important to know, however, that whatever it is that you desire to create, you must have a mental equivalent of it. Wayne Dyer, an American philosopher, self-help author, and motivational speaker would say it like this, "You'll see it when you believe it."

One of the most necessary things to remember is that we cannot demonstrate life beyond our ability to embody it. In other words, we cannot receive or manifest something if we have a belief that we are not worthy of or capable of having it. Having a mental equivalent of something and feeling and knowing the possibility of it is imperative.

Learning how to focus our thoughts and concentrate our efforts on the vision and what is important is crucial. We must be aligned mentally with our goals and where we want to be.

As we challenge personal boundaries, move out of our comfort zones, and get comfortable with being uncomfortable, we will begin to move the needle of possibility. Be aware that our ego/protective personality is designed to keep us extremely comfortable and safe, and has no regard for expansion, growth, and new experiences. If it were up to the protective personally, it would lock you in a box and you'd never experience anything outside of what you already know. In a world of infinite possibilities, that is a shallow version in the depth of what is possible.

Making time to get grounded and anchored in a vision that is inspired and joyful may seem foreign at first; however, as you create deliberate time for prayer, meditation, walks, yoga sessions, bike rides, and/or whatever it is for you that wakes you up and makes you come alive, make more time for that. What we believe we are worth is what we will attract into our lives.

Creating a clear mental picture and affirming the truth that we are supported by an infinite and infallible presence—believing and knowing that this is the truth and I am one with all that I desire—this is where the magic of life begins to reveal itself.

Contemplate this: Today, I affirm my good and I focus on everything that I have and that I am grateful for. I give thanks for everyone and everything that has contributed to my life and I focus on gratitude.

Notes and Reflections

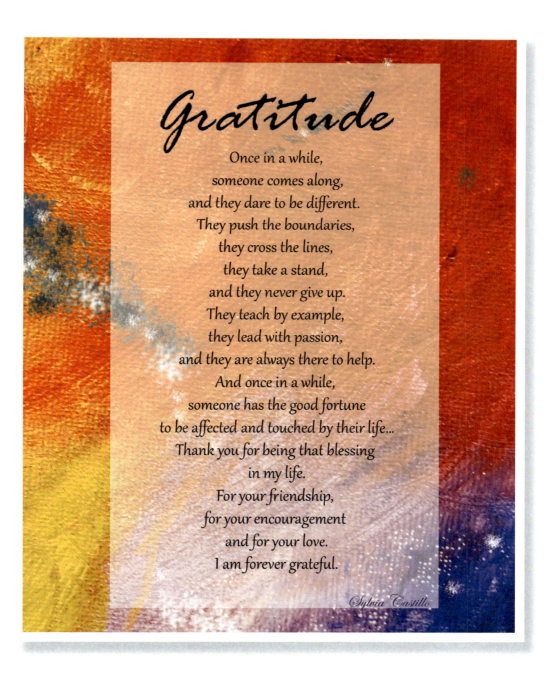

40. I will give all that I have to all that I am committed to

When we give all that we have to all that we are committed to, the results show for themselves. When we steward and focus our attention, time, energy, intention, and resources in the direction of our vision, there really is nothing and no one that can stand between us and our purpose.

When you make it your personal responsibility to give all that you have to all that you are committed to, remember to stay open. God, the Universe, Source, Spirit, whatever you call it, is conspiring for our greater good. And when we align with this truth, when we stay open at the top, meaning we don't judge where the flow of good can come from. We trust coincidental or chance meetings and introductions, we are positive about our good intentions and we have faith in what is not yet seen. When we operate from this perspective and when we make ourselves available to experience the joy, the reward, and the satisfaction of following our destiny, then we are on purpose.

This journey of self-reflection continues to be an opportunity to look in the mirror—to keep learning, growing, questioning, discovering, and re-committing.

I never thought that saying "yes" to those inner nudges and ideas would lead me here.

To have created Serenity's Way, a company that promotes messages of encouragement and empowerment, to write and teach a curriculum in the battered women's shelter, to support BTS (Break the Silence Against Domestic Violence) to fund and participate in their healing workshops, to be published in a bestselling book and now to have written my own book. I am committed to be the most authentic, real, open, and vulnerable woman that I can be, and somewhere along this path of growth, I decided that if someone else could benefit from things I've learned along the way, then I would make myself available to share what I've learned. My intention is to be a causal agent in healing the issue of domestic violence, and suffering in general. I understand the significance and power that each one of us has, and I am certain that you can never know the impact you will have on this world until you say yes.

So, what will you give yourself to? What will you be committed to so that when you leave this human experience you will feel that you left something behind that was worthy of you? The opportunity is to leave a legacy, to leave your imprint, your mark and your Spirit on what you feel called to do.

Sometimes the struggle of our own personal value comes up, and we question what it is that we have to give and/or contribute. However, when we continue on this path of growth, we recognize that leaving our contribution is actually the greatest gift that we have the opportunity to give. For some it feels like your soul's calling, and if you don't give or contribute to it, you may not see the purpose in life. If there is a feeling that something is missing or there is still something left to do—rest assured that you're not done yet. The best is yet to come and your clarity, focus, direction, and commitment will be needed.

If you are already giving all that you have, what does next level look like? Think about this: Today, I am open to the flow of creation. I surrender and release any thoughts that are not aligned with my highest vision. I know I am a causal agent in every experience of my life, and I am open to all of the good that is flowing to and through me.

Notes and Reflections

fly

Your dream is calling
with an invitation
to a brand new experience of life...
Patiently waiting for your permission
to own your gifts,
to accept your truth.
Longing for you to
step into the greatness of who you are,
and who you came here to be.
You have within you every resource you need-
the power, the intelligence, the skill,
the integrity, the heart
and the ability to soar into
the destiny that awaits you.
Say yes-
and choose this day
to make your dreams a reality.
You were born to fly~

Sylvia Castillo

41. I look for opportunities to give of myself, my time, and my service

The best medicine is being outwardly focused. When we look for opportunities to give of ourselves, our time and service, we have no idea how we impact the world on a larger scale. Every good deed, intention, hour, and energy given to make a difference, matters.

Have you ever noticed that it is just about impossible to be depressed, checked out, and distant when we are helping others? Maybe that's why so many people find it difficult to take care of themselves—because helping others gives us a feeling of worthiness and satisfaction of a job well done.

We all have something to contribute, and for many of us when we give back to a place in our lives where there has been pain and anguish, we offer compassion and understanding in a way that can never be found in a textbook or in theory. There is no schooling or education that offers the authenticity and humanity of real life experience.

If you have experienced a loss or a tragedy, and you feel alone in your grief, if you decide to reach out, you will find that there are others who feel the same. So often our pain is amplified in isolation and healing happens in community.

Interestingly enough, instead of the question being, "Why Me?" it becomes a statement of "I know your pain. I've been there, too". We have the opportunity to listen with ears of empathy, and we are able to offer such a sincere space that even the silence understands.

What you have to contribute is a gift to the world; maybe yours is a talent or a gift of your hands or mind. There are so many incredible voices, expressive dances, down home cooks, beautiful painters, and crafters. There are those who teach and council, preach and lend a hand. Maybe your gift is your kind heart and your gentle way of just being available? Whatever it is, it and you matter. When we Practice the Presence, meaning that when you use your soulful gift in service to others, that service is a blessing the world in ways that you cannot begin to image. It touches countless lives, because it lives on in those you touch as they pay it forward to others.

There is no substitute for the blessing of your gift or the gift of your time. There is also no check or amount of money that is an equivalent replacement. There is something about the human connection and about having the experience that a check just does not cover. It is also about the consistency. When we give our gifts on a consistent and regular basis, it is returned to us as a sense of peace and comfort in making a difference. There is a fulfillment and a sense of satisfaction; it is the reciprocal reward that leaves a lasting impression in our lives and on our hearts.

This is what it means to be the hands and feet, to decide to *be* the change, to make a difference, to give back, to stand up, and dig in. Find your people, your calling, tribe, circle, posse—or whatever you call it. Get involved and give of yourself. It's an immeasurable gift to your life, and you won't know to what extent until you say "yes" to the experience.

Affirm: Today, I acknowledge the gifts of contribution that are within me. I commit to finding a way to share, volunteer, and/or give back. I recognize that when I am outwardly focused, I make a difference.

Notes and Reflections

42. because I understand the dynamic exchange of giving and receiving, and the amazing blessings it brings to my life

There is a dynamic exchange of giving and receiving. It is never one sided, and it is always reciprocated. The interesting thing about giving is that you will probably not receive in the same place that you give. In other words, when you find yourself giving to your church or volunteer program, what you get in return may be in a completely different area of your life.

You might win a jackpot or receive an unexpected check in the mail. You could get the help you were needing, find a sale on an item you needed to purchase, or receive an opportunity that happened unexpectedly. Often times, we think these events are not related, and we may even make the statement that, "I don't get anything in return." However, when we release the need to keep score and just notice, we will see blessings of all kinds just showing up.

The opportunity is always to be the witness and to notice. As a spiritual practice, tithing is one way to activate the law of circulation. The law of circulation states that things in the universe are always flowing in circulation, but at an ever-expanding rate. It works according to the law of cause and effect—the universe always mirrors back to you whatever you do. Tithing is generally a practice of giving the first 10% of your earnings to the place and or person that lifts you up spiritually. If it's true that you get what you give, it might be a good idea to look at your giving.

For those that have negative energy around tithing or giving, this is an opportunity to create a different relationship with it. Tithing is about keeping an open channel of giving and receiving in your life. It's about giving first and knowing that in return you will be blessed.

There is purposefulness to you giving first in faith and knowing and trusting that it will be returned to you.

Imagine standing in front of an old fireplace; there is a stack of wood, matches, and newspaper all right there. Because you don't want to give first, you ask the fireplace to give you heat and then you will give it wood. You explain that because of your past experiences you'll need to see the fire before you can offer your wood. The fireplace tells you that you will need to be the first to give and to trust the process. It goes on to say that all of your resources are right there and that you just need to be the first one to give. Instead, you sit right down on the hearth in front of the fireplace and wrap another blanket around you.

There are so many areas of our lives where we withhold, waiting for someone or something else to give first because we don't want to lose out. Add to that the evidence of past hurts or experiences and we will hang on tight to the reasons why we're not going to give at all. Now tithing is in reference to money however, where else in your life are you withholding your forgiveness, trust, appreciation, love, friendship.

Since the opportunity is always to practice, let's start with tithing. The Unexpected Income Club is giving with money that was completely unexpected. This idea or practice is an invitation to really use your life as a laboratory. To explore ideas, concepts, and practices that you may have not known about or simply overlooked. This is an opportunity to make giving a priority because you are interested in experiencing for yourself the amazing blessings it returns.

In the Unexpected Income Club, you are consciously giving from the overflow you have in your life. It is money that you were not expecting and giving from it is a conscious choice to pay it forward. We hold an expectancy of good with the idea that it will be returned multiplied. For example, if you received a refund check in the mail of $100, you would give 10% ($10) to whatever cause or place that you consider your spiritual sustenance. Keep a record and pay attention to the blessings and miracles that simply show up.

This is an opportunity to get outside any limiting beliefs, and to consciously participate in practices that allow you to be mindful of what you are giving of your time, money and service. Today, say, I commit to give first.

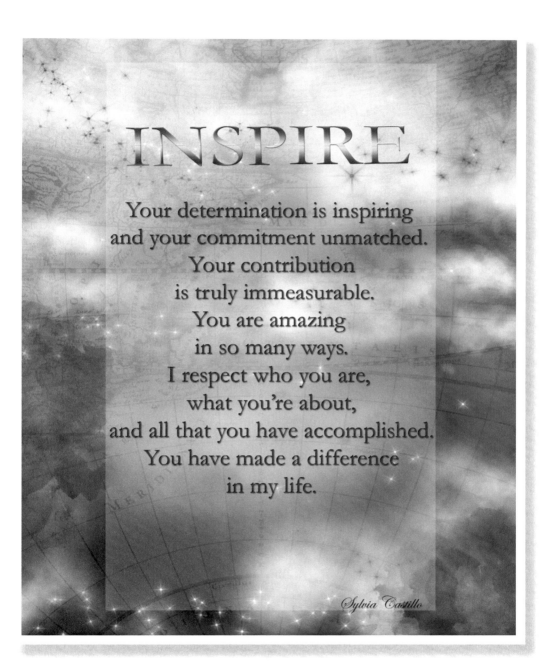

INSPIRE

Your determination is inspiring
and your commitment unmatched.
Your contribution
is truly immeasurable.
You are amazing
in so many ways.
I respect who you are,
what you're about,
and all that you have accomplished.
You have made a difference
in my life.

Sylvia Castillo

43. As I move into this day I carry with me these truths and agreements

As I move into this day, I am making a conscious commitment to carry with me and to be mindful of these truths and agreements and to use them in my daily life.

...

I am impeccable with my word, and I use my heart and intuition as my guidance.

I pay close attention to when listening is more important than being heard.

I recognize that the need to understand always takes precedence over the egos demands. I know that my character, my honesty, and my integrity are all defined by my word, so I don't make promises that I cannot keep. I am free to choose in every moment to respond instead of react, and I vow to never use my words as a weapon or an excuse.

I don't partake in rumors and gossip, for I absolutely know that there is no power or personal growth in the depreciation of another.

I don't take things personally, I recognize that we are all on a journey—learning, growing, discovering, finding, reaching and figuring out our own plan. When I stay committed to my highest vision, when I am in integrity with myself, I approach others with patience and humility. I know that each of us is doing the best we can with our current level of awareness, and I honor that space. I release all demands and expectations that keep me in judgment, and I forgive myself and others for our misgivings.

I don't assume anything. I accept full and total responsibility for my life, for my relationships, and for my results. If there is something I need to know, I ask. If there is something I need to say, I communicate. If there is something missing, I do the best I can to articulate and express who and what I am, and what it is that I need or desire. There is no story writing; I will not create my own doubt, animosity, confusion, illusion, bitterness, suspicion or conflict based on speculation. I am clear and conscious—I use my time, my energy and my voice for resolution and solution. I am committed to greatness.

I will do the best I can, and I start with me. I will love, honor, and nurture myself. I will take care of my needs, protect my space, expand my consciousness, exercise my body, and shape my life. I will give time to the things that inspire and bring joy to me. I will give all that I have to all that I am committed to. I will look for opportunities to give of myself, my time, and my service because I understand the dynamic exchange of giving and receiving, and the amazing blessings it brings to my life.

....

I am recognizing that I am the common denominator wherever I go. I know that as I work on my mindset, as I cultivate my ability to respond, and as I continue to be the best possible version of myself that I can be. I am creating my path of happiness, abundance and prosperity in every way.

Notes and Reflections

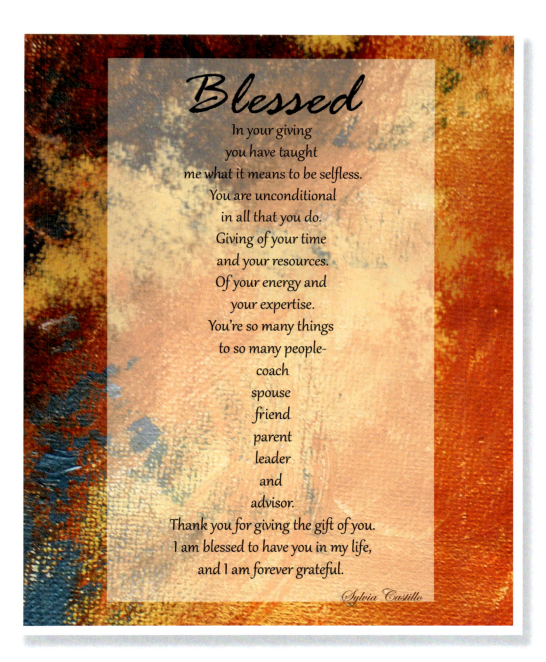

44. and I remember to be gentle along the way

Of all things, remember to be gentle along the way. As you are making your way, be mindful of those around you. Your light and your consciousness are needed. Your positivity, enthusiasm, encouragement, and the desire to be a better person are essential. When you live from these agreements and when you are outwardly focused, you give yourself to the world in an inspiring way that allows others to do the same.

Imagine a world where we are all important, where no one is left out. Where everyone matters, and we are all equal. Imagine that your gentleness and loving nature actually alters the way that you interact with others.

Your curiosity and interest in experiencing new and lasting relationships and results will positively affect how you think of others. When we decide to approach others with genuine interest and a loving presence regardless of how they show up, we will change the frequency of that interaction. If we deeply understood that their pain is related to their perception, we can and will alter outcomes with our BEingness. It sounds too good to be true, and yet, it is the opportunity that each of us has.

Remember to do unto others as you would have done unto you. Often times we are in overdrive, working with the busyness of everyday life, and yet, if we could hit pause or slow down to breathe and take notice, we will see opportunities all around us to be gentler, kinder, and more compassionate. Remember to be compassionate with yourself as well, although it is sometimes easier to think of others before yourself. You have to remember to give from your overflow. You cannot give what you do not have.

There is something about this image of perfection where we think that we have to have it all done just right. Often times we forget to be gentle with ourselves. We berate and belittle in a way that is completely disempowering. It's really time to let it go and to practice being in the moment.

Today, I decide to be in harmony. In a world where we can choose to be anything, I choose to be kind. I choose to be thoughtful and deliberate, and I choose to love unconditionally.

Notes and Reflections

harmony

Let ease and grace
guide your affairs.
Let all of your decisions
be influenced
by your inner wisdom.
Let your heart be filled with unconditional love.
Drop in and allow this place of certainty
to anchor in,
to absolutely know
that you are here·
purposefully and powerfully.
Let this be your truth
today and always...

Sylvia Castillo

45. I remember that life is always offering up the opportunity for me to be, do, and have everything I desire

Life is meant to flow, and as we let go of what it's supposed to look like. As we continue to forgive and release all of our demands and expectations of others—as we focus on our vision and allow things to unfold naturally—we will experience what we call miracles.

There are no coincidences; there is, however, the opportunity to recognize that life is lining up in accordance and in alignment to our beliefs. We came here to have an *Experience of Love*. Because we came from love and because we will return to love, this human experience is the only opportunity we have to *feel it*. And, we can actually change the direction of a relationship or circumstance with our own personal commitment to create new results.

My friend Larry was in a new marriage, and he wanted desperately to have different results than that of his previous relationship. Larry was noticing that as much as he wanted things to be different, they weren't. He seemed to be having the same types of challenges as he did previously, and it was devastating. He believed his new marriage was the relationship of his dreams, and he wanted so much to not repeat some of the same mistakes and patterns he had created in the past. My question to Larry was, "How committed will you be in your moments of frustration"? I encouraged him to be mindful of his responses. My ongoing observation was that it was easy for things to be great when everyone is happy. What happens in those moments when you want to fire back or get angry? When you feel like you're losing control and you have the desire to defend yourself. It is in these precious seconds (and it's literally seconds) that we have an opportunity to take a deep breath and anchor into our bigger vision. Consciously choosing to respond instead of having that same knee-jerk reaction that is usually followed with regret and apologies.

The opportunity for Larry to be do and have everything he desired is created by him—because of his commitment to show up differently so that he would create new and results in his life.

My own experience of this was when I literally stopped a conversation short of a train wreck. Steve and I were just getting ready for bed and something he said hit me wrong. I got up to use the restroom and immediately thought of all of the things I was going to say to defend myself. I was upset and frustrated, and I just knew it was going to be a big argument. And then in just a fleeting second, I remembered to be the witness. I decided in that moment to just lay down my defenses and approach the remark from curiosity. I thought about what I could do to be humble, and I grabbed the lotion to rub his feet and decided to ask him to help me understand his comment. That shift in my own awareness created a completely different outcome. Instead of an argument, we had an intimate, loving and thoughtful experience.

Life is giving us the opportunity daily to create a new outcome; however, it doesn't always look like what we think. It is our responsibility to do the work in the in-between moments. To do our meditation, prayer, breathwork, yoga, or whatever practice so that we are living with awareness and with one eye on the inside, all of the time. Then, when those challenging moments come up, we will have the wherewithal to stop, take a deep breath, and decide how to respond. There is no flashing warning light that says, "Ok, here it comes. You better get ready. Here's that moment." It will be a feeling in the body that we have named anger, anxiety, fear, frustration, and so on. It is actually coming up to the surface to be healed, and we can either respond as usual or decide in that moment to choose something different.

When we choose to BE love and to BE present in these moments, we are creating a new path for our lives. When we believe that life is for us and not against us, it really gives us the opportunity to perceive change from the idea of possibility (love) rather than impossibility (fear).

If I lose my job and I have a possibility perspective, I see that loss as a blessing and an opportunity to have a new experience, to make more money, learn a new trade, meet more people, etc. If I have a perspective of impossibility or fear, I will be angry, resentful, and doubtful of myself, my circumstances, and my future.

Now, here's the interesting thing: if life is *always* responding to us in accordance with our beliefs to give us more of what we think we are (and it is), what place is going to serve my highest good? Love or fear?

Say out loud: Today, I am intentional in all that I do.

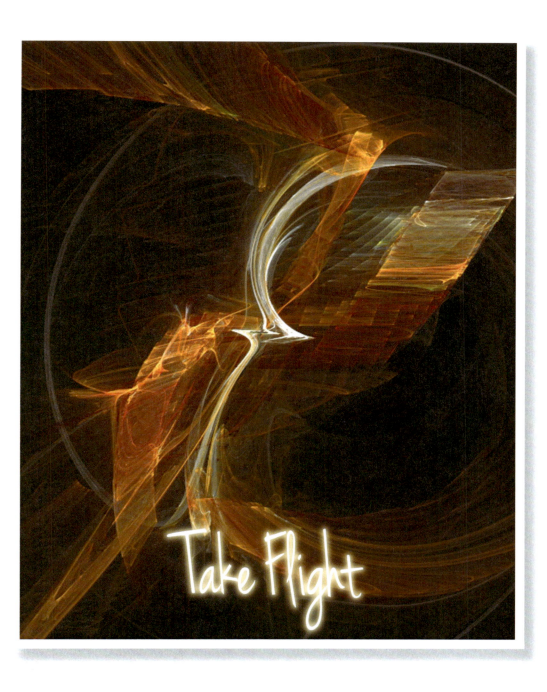

46. I choose yes and let it be so

To choose yes is to acknowledge that you are always at choice, and that you make a choice to say "yes" to a journey of self-love and discovery. This is such a statement of power. The exploration of personal development is not for the weary. It is humbling to look in the mirror for the purpose of growth. And, it is here where we observe what gets us excited about life, it is here where we decide who and what we will give our time and attention to and what attitudes and behaviors are outdated, what no longer serves the larger vision for our lives and what will be done different today.

Choosing "yes" can be a moment-by-moment decision, and as we keep practicing, observing, and being the witness, it becomes easier and easier to stay in alignment with the people and circumstances where we feel like we are in the flow of life.

A lot of times, we use the phrase "I have to." "I have to go to work, pick up the kids, make dinner…" the list goes on and on. What if instead we said, "I get to," as though it was a choice that we have said yes to. There is so much power and personal responsibility in saying "yes" or "no" and meaning it, and we are always at choice. We are not bound or chained to any person, situation, commitment, or chore. We have a choice, and to be in alignment with our choices, to feel good about the choices we are making, is to make good use of the free will that we all have.

Remember Jessica? She was in the midst of a Transformation when she decided to leave her marriage. Jessica said "yes" to a larger vision for her life—to growth and expansion in ways she knew were possible and had yet to experience. Her vision and the "yes" to the vision—to believe and then see, is exactly what she did. Jessica left an unfulfilled marriage to rise up to meet a vision she knew was possible. Today, she is happily remarried to an incredible man, her coaching business is thriving, she has a beautiful home, amazing stepchildren and a life that she had imagined was possible. She is living her dream and helping other people find theirs. And, because she consciously uncoupled, she also kept her friendship with her ex-husband, and they continue to run their previous transaction management business together. She turned impossible into absolutely.

There are no limitations. We are not bound by anything other than our own beliefs about what is possible. Once those thoughts, ideas, beliefs, and feelings are shifted into possibility things will change. We can create, renew, and restore any relationship, passion, idea, or dream. What we focus on expands, what we believe we see, what we give to grows, and we absolutely do create our own reality. So, Let It percolate, Let It rise up, Let It be discovered, Let It be declared, and Let It Be So!

Notes and Reflections

47. And So It Is

And So It Is—this is a declaration. It is an announcement, a positive formal statement and proclamation. The process of this chapter in the book of your life is complete.

What you choose to carry with you will alter the rest of your path. There are so many opportunities to look within to learn and uncover, so much revealed and healed. You are loved and forgiven; the process is complete. Whatever it was that needed to be learned is learned, whatever needed to be released is released.

At the end of the day and at the end of this life's journey, you being authentically you is all that really matters. No one is going to tell you that you did it wrong. No one is going to lock you out of heaven or send you to a fiery hell. We will all return to the love that created us.

I hope that you are done waiting and that you are ready to live the life you came here to create. I hope that you continue to discover, commit, and to express as only you can. I know that you are open to every gift and every experience of a larger life and that it is already done. Remember to celebrate and acknowledge yourself. This has been an incredible journey of self-discovery and movement, and you deserve to be recognized, even if it's just you toasting to the best that is yet to come.

48. What's next

What's next? What does continuing this journey of personal development look like? This is not a one and done; it is a lifelong journey and adventure. There is not one class, seminar, workshop, message, guru, or teacher that has all of the answers. So, what's next? It is important that you continue to cultivate the garden of your life. Because life is always a process of becoming, there is no arrival, there is always something we can learn about ourselves.

Remember to pay attention to how you feel. When we are in alignment with what is good and true, we *feel* energized, awake, aware, and alive. We are inspired from a place within, more than being motivated from the outside, we are guided and inspired from the inside. It is a personal journey in which we all get to brings our gifts, talents, cooperation, joy, and enthusiasm to to the experience.

Bask in the glory; allow yourself the space to feel amazing about what you learned and what you've created and accomplished. Decide how you will continue to implement these new-found ideas, and watch how things in your life begin to shift and change.

Then, when it's time for more, say "yes" and begin again. There are so many opportunities to learn and grow from in this world. So many incredible people who have given their life to teach what they know, and it is so good.

When we are influenced by Source, we elicit acceptance, love, kindness, and compassion. Imagine what you can be created when we make it a point to stay under the influence of unconditional love. I hope that whatever is next in your journey, you take this knowing with you.

Included in this book is a resource page. It will outline the people and programs that have assisted me in my own process of growth and expansion. I invite you to take a look or to find something else that lights you up and continues to inspire your life.

Notes and Reflections

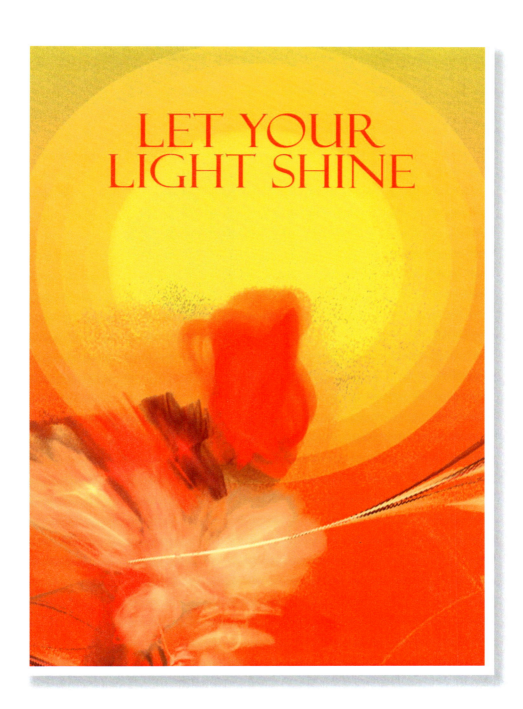

49. Conclusion ~ a Divine message to take with you

My greatest desire is that you come to know and love yourself.

There is only light and there is only love. It is warm, it is tender, and it is safe.

In this moment you fully recognize, you sense that place of perfection within.

It is calling you, calling you to remember. And as you surrender, as you let go you, as you embrace this moment, in all of its fullness listen to these words…

My beautiful child, my light of the world. I cherish these moments with you, I cherish these times when you consciously and knowingly decide to take a moment and surrender. When you come home to the truth, when you go within. When you take a moment to stand still and stand in your truth. I cherish these moments when you sense that place of perfection within you, as you remember your wholeness.

Remember today that you are here on purpose; remember that there is nothing standing between you and your truth. I created you in my image—perfect, whole, and complete.

I created you to grow, to play, to love, and to laugh. I created you to be a vessel of kindness and compassion. To live fully—with abundance, peace, and prosperity.

You are the light of the world; you are moving and growing and expanding in your consciousness.

Love surrounds you in each and every moment. You are divinely guided, you are nurtured, and you are blessed. You are energized and revitalized in this precious and sacred moment. Remember always that you need only say "yes."

There is a place inside of you that is calling—and it is calling on purpose. Listen to it; it is drawing to you everything you need for a more expansive life; it is calling you to grow and to become. It is calling you to step into your greatness. It is calling you because you are needed, because you are the one. There is nothing and no one else. It is calling you by name because it is your unique gift. It is you and only you.

And as you move beyond your human fears, as you move in faith, you will see that you've never been lost, nor alone, nor forsaken.

You are love, you are light, and you are perfect in every way. I have given you the heavens, and today, my sweet child, embrace this moment, as you fully remember.

Today, you are inspired, you are activated, motivated, and you move beyond any doubt, and confusion, or any circumstance. In this moment, your destiny awaits you. Your every need, every resource, and every activity are in divine flow. With love, peace, ease, and grace, miracles are manifesting in this and each and every moment.

As you continue on your journey, know that I am always with you. My beautiful child, I am always with you…

Notes and Reflections

It's because you are loved,
because I care about who you
are and who you become.
It's because you bring love and joy to my life
like no one else can.
It's because you are uniquely and beautifully
and wonderfully you.
It's because in so many ways
you teach and inspire me
and because without you,
my life would never be the same...

Sylvia Castillo

50. A New Vision

The invitation is to keep expanding on the vision for your life. Who are you now and what will you choose to deliberately create?

Vision

I give thanks for this new perspective,
as I take responsibility
for right here and right now.
I recognize that life was simply waiting for me...
No longer am I willing to compromise
my personal integrity.
No longer am I willing to sabotage
my dreams and desires.
No longer am I willing to
pretend that I am not enough.
Today I step into
a new reality and
a brand new vision for my life.
I give thanks for every circumstance and
situation that made me who I am,
and I move into every
tomorrow with a new found
Yes for life.

Sylvia Castillo

51. No Arrival

There is no arrival and in this game of life. We are always choosing how we will play. We know now that we choose from our directive power—because we have dominion over our thoughts and because we are always at choice. As you begin to live your life from True Choice, I invite you to consider noticing the people around you and to make a conscious decision to help lift them up. To make a difference where you can and to play your part.

> *"Life is a game and you are the player.*
> *As you master the game,*
> *so you also create it."*
> *—Jay Woodman*

True Choice

Playing to Win. Comes from I want to. I'm going to win attitude. Takes personal responsibility for the choices they make, good or bad. Solution oriented, pro-active, always working on their attitude, always looking for solutions. Supportive of others despite how they show up. Always taking action on their goals and excited about getting them. Supports others and comes from essence.

False Choice

Playing not to lose. Come from I have to. Doesn't feel excited about getting goals because they question their integrity or reason for getting their goals. Gets exhausted, feels contradiction because they don't want people to know how they really feel. Bulldoze their way through because its expected, because they're supposed to, and there is a need to look good. I said, "I'm going to do it, so I'm going to do it." In false choice, people are reactive and feel defensive.

Avoid Choice

Just Playing. Have a choice, but don't make it. Usually, if they don't make a choice, it's made for them, and it's not the choice they want or when they want it. Spectator attitude. Wait and see; meanwhile, they are righteous and defensive "Don't tell me what to do." They are confused a lot, which is also a choice to avoid. This is where the masses of people live and operate from.

Deny Choice.

Not Playing. See themselves as having no responsibility and go to blame so they can never fail. It's always "out there." Denies ownership so they cannot fail, and they keep themselves separate. Victim Consciousness, denying that they have a choice in life.

When we take the time to do this work we can see that it really is about the perspective we have. We've learned that with awareness, a shift in our thought processes, a commitment to prayer and meditation, pluse some body and breathwork, it is absolutely possible to change and create a new reality.

Today, I am outwardly focused. I recognize that not everyone is living from True Choice. Wherever I can build a bridge, be of service, lend a helping hand, give a hug, or make a difference, I do that.

Notes and Reflections

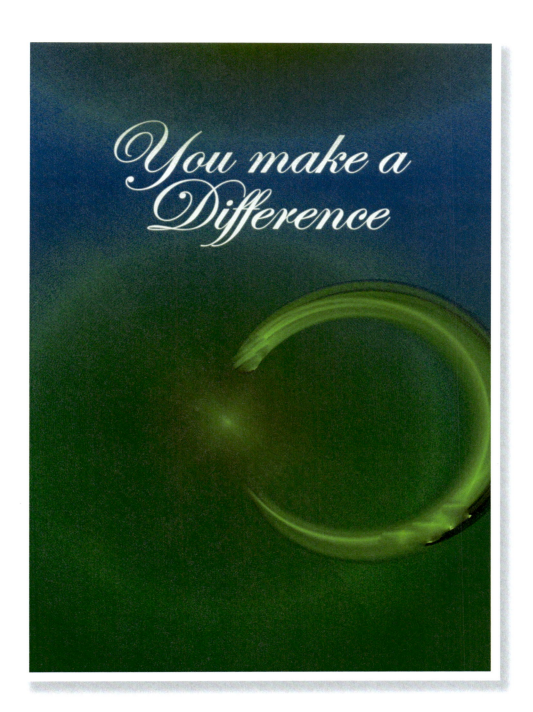

Resources

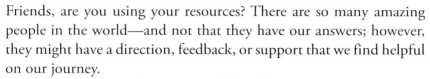

Friends, are you using your resources? There are so many amazing people in the world—and not that they have our answers; however, they might have a direction, feedback, or support that we find helpful on our journey.

As always, I strongly recommend that if you do not have a spiritual home, you find one. Make sure that it aligns with your beliefs and values and that you feel great about the message it teaches. Above all, make sure it is all inclusive and leaves no one out. We are sisters and brothers in one human family, and the more we align with that truth, the less we have a need be against one another. Remember that addiction happens in isolation and recovery happens in community. Let's continue to build our communities.

These resources have been instrumental and have greatly contributed to my life. If you are looking for a place to start and need some resources, here are my recommendations:

RESOURCES

Books

Breaking the Habit of Being Yourself	Dr Joe Despenza
Brilliant Babies Powerful Adults	John and Susan Mike MD
Never in Your Wildest Dreams	Natalie Ledwell
Seven Spiritual Laws of Success	Deepak Chopra
The Magic & The Secret	Rhonda Byrne
This Thing Called You	Ernest Holmes
This Life is Joy	Dr Roger Teel
The Energy Codes	Dr Sue Morter

Teachings/Teachers
Abraham-Esther Hicks   www.abraham-hicks.com
Dr Sue Morter   www.drsuemorter.com
Mile Hi Church   www.milehichurch.org
PSI Seminars   www.PSISeminars.com

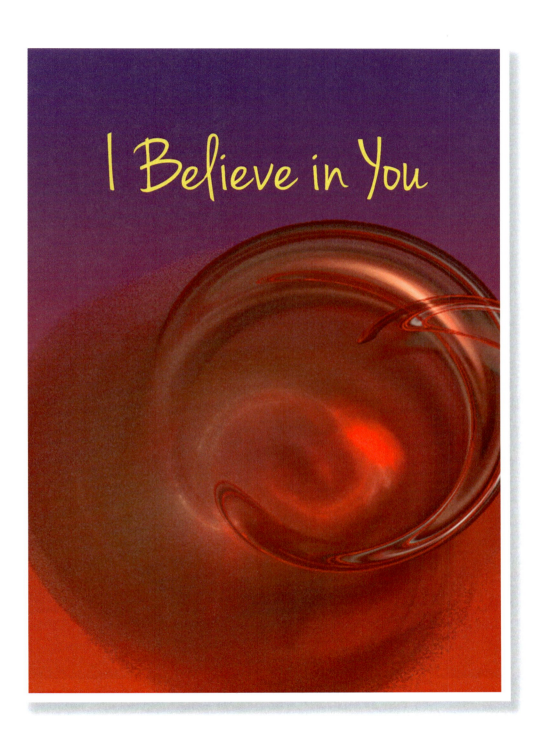

Closing Thoughts

My heart is full. As I type out these last few thoughts, I am overwhelmed with emotion at the possibility that your life was touched by taking this journey.

My intention has only been for good; it is from the belief and knowingness that we are all brothers and sisters in one human family, and that our ultimate gift is the giving and receiving of our unconditional love.

I hope that you continue to create amazing results in your life and more importantly, I hope you take time to go within, that you would be still and know…

Know that you get to create your life, you will always be enough, you are perfect, whole, and complete, you are forgiven, and you are unconditionally loved.

Sending you lots of love as
you embrace your truth~

Acknowledgements

There are so many people that have touched my heart and who have added so much to my life experience. For my immediate and extended family, I am grateful for your continued support and encouragement. For Scott and Lora Nordby who introduced me to personal development and gave me a work environment where I couldn't help but to grow, thank you. You both have been a blessing in my life and I will always be grateful for you. For author and Real Estate expert Larry Kendall, who asked me to write a piece for his book Ninja Selling. Writing the Ninja Prayer ignited a fire within me and your belief in me meant more than you could ever know. For all of my Practitioner friends who hold the high watch for all of us, I am grateful for you. For all of my PSI friends, you know who you are and there are too many to list here. For the teaching team on the *My Agreements with Me* video podcast journey, Karisa Bieglow, Darice Johnston Brown, Deanne Drda MA, Laura Jacob, Jessica & Rodd Jaramillo, Sherri Overstreet, Audrey May-Prosper, Terri Wiber, and Kathy Sparrow, who is also my editor—your contribution, individually and collectively was such a selfless gift. Our conversations added so much value to The Journey. I am grateful for your presence in my life and I love and admire each one of you. For Honeylette Pino who created the layout and design for the book and who also added to the cover, you made it easy and I appreciated the help. For Scott and Marla Wynn, who so serendipitously showed up in my life at just the right time, and who's technical and creative insight made the online journey a reality, thank you. And, for my mom— I dedicated my first cards, the Women's Empowerment Series to you. That series and this book is about the strength in every one of us. Thank you for giving me your strength and all that you endured for us, I know you did the best you could and I love you.

About the Author

I am committed to growth, learning and personal development. Having grown up in motels with domestic violence as a way of life, I often wondered what life was really about and always felt that there had to be more than what I was experiencing.

I often felt like I didn't belong, I looked for ways to escape a feeling of unworthiness, and oftentimes that meant making choices that were far off of any moral compass.

Like many others that are brought up in environments lacking conscious conversations, emotional support, and guidelines and boundaries- I began to search for my own answers.

My personal development began with PSI Seminars and for more than a decade I consumed myself with books, classes, coaching, events and workshops for my own growth and expansion.

The teachers I most resonated with were Dr Sue Morter, Abraham Hicks, Rev. Michael Beckwith, Dr. Roger Teel, Deepak Chopra, Oprah Winfrey and many others that influenced my life.

In 2012, I was Licensed as a Practitioner (RScP) for the Centers for Spiritual Living. In 2013, I created SerenitysWay, an affirmative greeting card company. It was here that I wanted to leave a message for someone who needed to hear the words—"You are worthy. You are enough. Your past does not preceed you. You matter, and you are not alone."

What I deeply recognize is that regardless of our upbringing, we all have "stuff" and how we interpret it and what we do with it, will dictate our actions, affect our results and alter the rest of our lives.

My husband and children (Steve, Taylor, Dante, Kamryn and Baileigh) will tell you that I am no guru, I certainly have never claimed to be. They are my tribe, and I so love and appreciate each one of them for who they are and for supporting me all of these years to follow my path.

I continue to evolve and to continue to work on being the best version of myself that I can possibly be. I don't think that journey ever ends, it is an inside job and it is a lifelong opportunity. Here's to all of us on the path.